OUR LIFE AFTER DEATH

OUR LIFE AFTER DEATH

A Firsthand Account
from an 18th-Century Scientist and Seer

EMANUEL SWEDENBORG

Translated by George F. Dole
Introduction by Kenneth Ring

SWEDENBORG FOUNDATION
West Chester, Pennsylvania

First printing 2013
Revised second printing 2014

This volume contains a modified version of text originally
published in Emanuel Swedenborg's *Heaven and Hell*, as
translated by George F. Dole in the New Century Edition of the
Works of Emanuel Swedenborg (West Chester, PA: Swedenborg
Foundation, 2000). It is excerpted from material in that volume
titled "The World of Spirits and Our State after Death" (sections
421–535) and "Children in Heaven" (sections 329–345).

The introduction by Kenneth Ring was originally published in
Awaken from Death (San Francisco: J. Appleseed & Co., 1993) and is
reprinted with permission.

Edited by Stuart Shotwell
Design and typesetting by Karen Connor

Printed in the United States of America

Swedenborg Foundation
320 North Church Street • West Chester, PA 19380
www.swedenborg.com

The Swedenborg Foundation
dedicates this volume to
Dick and Sally Brickman
in deep gratitude for their
vision, passion, and support.

CONTENTS

INTRODUCTION

There are of course many paths that lead up to the summit of Emanuel Swedenborg's sweeping spiritual vision of the life beyond. In my case, I came to discover Swedenborg through my research into near-death experiences (NDEs)—those compelling revelations, occurring on the threshold of apparent imminent death, that appear to usher individuals into a realm of transcendent beauty where time dissolves into eternity and God's light is everywhere. Even before I came to see the unmistakable parallels between the world Swedenborg had described for us more than two centuries ago and that which contemporary near-death experiencers were being vaulted into as a result of some kind of near-death crisis, others had already made this connection clear. Indeed, the first, and still in many ways the best, book to be written on the near-death experience in our own time, *Life After Life* by Raymond A. Moody, Jr., contained a section where those parallels were explicitly discussed. In it, Moody highlighted Swedenborg's teachings concerning what happens at the moment of death—and afterward. My appreciation of Swedenborg's writings has from the beginning been filtered through and indeed enhanced by my study of near-death experiences and my pondering of their obvious implications both for life after and *before* death.

The book you now hold in your hands is in fact one that, by drawing from Swedenborg's best-known and enduringly popular work on this subject, *Heaven and Hell,* provides an excellent introduction to Swedenborg's vision and understanding of the life beyond. As one quickly learns, this rendering is not one that stems from theological dogma but is, rather, rooted in Swedenborg's own personal and extraordinary sojourns into the spiritual world itself. His revelations, however, do not derive from the kind of brief glimpses that near-death experiencers have often reported to me and other NDE researchers, but from sustained and deliberate forays into this domain. As Swedenborg himself says, he was not merely told but *shown* through direct experience what the dying person encounters, both at the moment of physical death and afterward, and he was enabled to have such experiences frequently over the last third of his lifetime, a period of nearly three decades. Thus Swedenborg is hardly just a precursor to today's NDEers; he is a true seer and, as such, he had already mapped the realm that NDE research has tried to sketch out with its own methods.

What is the nature of this world? Here, Swedenborg makes it plain, we enter into a domain where the "essence" of ourselves is disclosed, and where we—and others—see ourselves with razor-sharp precision for who we really are. Death changes nothing, but reveals everything about us. This is just one of the many points of correspondence between Swedenborg's teachings and the findings of NDE research, by the way, which indicates that many persons have a detailed "life review" in which they are led to see not merely how they have lived, but the inner meaning and motivations of their actions, and the effects of those actions upon others. At death, we enter a world where, in short, our inner essence becomes "the environment" in which we find ourselves. In the end, Swedenborg says, "everyone returns after death to his own life." A person who has lived a life of self-centered cruelty finds himself continuing to live that way, far from the light of God. On the other hand, a person who has truly lived for others and for whom the existence of the Divine is at the heart of his life, is already in heaven, Swedenborg asserts, and continues to experience directly the Light of heaven after death and to find himself in the company of like-minded others. Either way, according to Swedenborg, everyone "is going to be an image of his affection, or his love." So it is, if we follow Swedenborg's teachings, that we are building our heaven and hell now, and living in them now, too, depending on the inner meaning of our actions in the world.

This, to me, is the great moral lesson in Swedenborg's vision of the afterlife—and it is one that once again coincides with the moral implications of NDEs: as the beloved Sufi poet Kabir has it, "what is found now is found then." Near-death experiencers emphasize the importance of being involved with the world, not withdrawing from it; of serving others and not merely paying lip service to traditional religious pieties; of knowing, with certainty, that God exists and that there is a life after death. For them, it is their NDEs that have made plain the undeniable truth of these things. Yet Swedenborg was enabled to see all this, and so much beyond this, through his incomparable experiences in the spiritual realm. And because of his remarkable intellect and powers of expression, his writings, as excerpted in this book, contain a depth of wisdom and understanding that no modern NDEer could ever hope to match. Which is why I say the study of NDEs only leads up to Swedenborg's world—it can scarcely begin to suggest its compass.

Yet NDE research is, I think, for contemporary students of Swedenborg an important confirmation of his insights into the afterlife. During Swedenborg's own lifetime, and certainly afterward, there were many who dismissed his supposed visions, even while acknowledging that he had exceptional psychic or clairvoyant powers. Some, of course, thought him quite mad. However, in the light of NDEs—and literally millions of persons across the globe have had these experiences—it is no longer possible to deny that Swedenborg's visions have a definite experiential foundation. Too many people have seen what Swedenborg did—if not so far—and have drawn essentially the same conclusions as he did, for it to be tenable to explain away his experiences as merely some kind of idiosyncratic fancy or morbid hallucination. It is ironic that while many world-famous figures have of course long honored Swedenborg and recognized his greatness, it is the collective testimony of millions of ordinary men and women who have described what it is like to die that is helping to bring his sobering yet inspiring vision of life after death to many new readers today.

The Swedenborg Foundation has provided a real service in compiling this volume, which will now introduce you directly to some of the essential writings of Emanuel Swedenborg on life after death. May it be a spur to you to examine further the works of this spiritual genius.

—KENNETH RING
Author of *Life at Death* and *Heading Toward Omega*

EDITOR'S NOTE

This volume presents an excerpt from Emanuel Swedenborg's timeless classic, *Heaven and Hell*. Written more than two hundred years before Raymond A. Moody's *Life After Life* launched the study of near-death experiences, *Heaven and Hell* describes, from the point of view of a firsthand investigator, our passing to the spiritual world after death and the shape of our life there. Since its initial publication in 1758, it has inspired countless thinkers, writers, and artists. Some scholars see it as forming one of the crucial links between the Enlightenment and Romanticism.

This version is based on the translation by George F. Dole, originally published in the Swedenborg Foundation's New Century Edition of the Works of Emanuel Swedenborg. The focus of this edited version has been to expand the terms that readers usually find difficult in Swedenborg and to represent the clarity of Swedenborg's thought in each sentence, rather than to preserve a level of diction identical to his. The resulting version has been rechecked against the Latin at each step of the way to ensure that the text does not stray from Swedenborg's original meaning.

For this edited version, some passages within Swedenborg's original chapters have been omitted or rearranged. In a very few instances, the material in some sentences has been condensed. These omissions and rearrangements have not been indicated in the text. Readers who find this sample of Swedenborg's work intriguing are invited to read the full version in *Heaven and Hell*.

OUR LIFE AFTER DEATH

WHAT THE WORLD OF SPIRITS IS

The world of spirits is neither heaven nor hell but a place or a state of being between the two. It is where we first arrive after death. From there in due course we are either raised into heaven or thrown into hell, depending on how we have lived in this world.

It became clear to me that it is a halfway place when I saw that the hells were underneath it and the heavens above it, and that it is a halfway state of being when I learned that as long as we are in it, we are not yet in either heaven or hell.

In the following pages, where I say "spirits," I mean people in the world of spirits; while by "angels" I mean people in heaven.

There is a vast number of people in the world of spirits, because that is where everyone is first gathered and where everyone is examined and prepared. There is no fixed limit to our stay there. Some people barely enter it and are promptly either taken up into heaven or thrown down into hell. Some stay there for only a few weeks, others for a number of years, though not more than thirty. The variations in the length of our stay occur because of the correspondence or lack of correspondence between our deeper and our outer natures.

In the following pages I will be explaining just how we are prepared and led from one state of being into another.

After we die, just as soon as we arrive in the world of spirits, we are carefully sorted out by the Lord. Evil people are immediately connected with the hellish community their ruling love had affiliated them with in the world, and good people are immediately connected with the heavenly community their love and kindness and faith had affiliated them with in the world.

Even though we are sorted out in this way, we are still together in that world and can talk to anyone when we want to, to friends and acquaintances from our physical life, especially husbands and wives, and also brothers and sisters. I have seen a father recognizing and talking with his six sons. I have seen many other people with their relatives and friends. However, since they differed in character because of their life in the world, they parted company after a little while.

However, people who go into heaven from the world of spirits do not see people who go into hell, and vice versa. Nor do those in each group recognize the others in it unless they have a similar character because of a similarity in what they love. The reason they can see these other people when they are in the world of spirits but not when they are in heaven or hell is that while they are in the world of spirits they are brought into states of being like those they were in during their physical lives, one after another. After a while, though, they settle into a constant state of being that agrees with the state of their ruling love. In this state of being, people recognize others only if what they love is similar, since similarity unites and dissimilarity separates.

Just as the world of spirits is a state of being halfway between heaven and hell, it is also a halfway place, as I mentioned earlier. The hells are underneath it and the heavens above it.

All the hells are closed on the side that faces that world, and are accessible only through holes and crevices like those in rocks and through broad gaps that are guarded to prevent anyone from coming out without permission, which is granted only in cases of real need. Heaven, too, is bounded on all sides, and the only access to any heavenly community is by a narrow way whose entry is also guarded. These exits and entrances are what are called the doors and gates of hell and heaven in the Word.

The world of spirits looks like a valley surrounded by mountains and cliffs, with glens and rising ground here and there. The doorways and entrances to heavenly communities become visible only to people who have been readied for heaven, and no one else finds them. There is one entrance going from the world of spirits to each community, and beyond that there is only one path; but as the path goes upward, it splits into many.

The doorways and gates to the hells are visible only to the people who are about to enter them. The gates open for them, and then they can see dark, sooty-looking caves slanting downward into the depths, where there are still more gates. Rank, foul stenches breathe out from them. Good spirits flee from these odors because they are repelled by them, but evil spirits are drawn toward them because they find them enjoyable. In fact, just as we enjoy our own evil in this world, we find enjoyment after death in the stench that corresponds to our evil. This can be compared to the enjoyment shown by carrion birds and beasts, such as crows and wolves and pigs, which fly or run toward rotting corpses as soon as they get wind of them. I heard one man who screamed aloud in utter torment at a breath of air from heaven, but was calm and happy when a breath from hell reached him.

There are two doors, so to speak, within each of us as well, one facing hell and open to evil and false things from there, the other facing heaven and open to good and true things from there. The door to hell is opened for people who focus on what is evil and on the falsity that comes from evil, though just a little light from heaven flows in through certain cracks, which enables us to think, reason, and speak. On the other hand, the door to heaven is opened for people who focus on what is good and thus on what is true. There are actually two paths that lead to our rational mind, one from above the mind or from inside it, through which goodness and truth enter from the Lord, and one from below the mind or from outside it, through which evil and falsity infiltrate from hell. The rational mind itself is in the middle, where these two paths meet; so the more light from heaven is let in, the more rational we are, and the more that light is shut out, the less rational we are, however the situation may appear to us.

I have mentioned these things so that our correspondence with heaven and with hell may be known. While our rational mind is in the process of being formed, it corresponds to the world of spirits. What is above it belongs to heaven, and what is beneath it belongs to hell. In people who are being readied for heaven, the higher aspects of the mind open, and the lower close against the inflow of evil and falsity. In people who are being readied for hell, the lower aspects open, and the higher close against the inflow of goodness and truth. As a result, the latter people can look only downward, toward hell, and the former people can look only upward, toward heaven. Looking upward is looking toward the Lord, because he is the common center that everything in heaven faces. Looking downward, though, is looking away from the Lord toward the opposite center, the center toward which everything in hell faces and gravitates.

EACH OF US IS INWARDLY A SPIRIT

Anyone who thinks things through carefully can see that it is not the body that thinks, because the body is material. Rather, it is the soul, because the soul is spiritual. The human soul, whose immortality has been the topic of many authors, is our spirit; it is in fact immortal in all respects, and it is also what does the thinking in our bodies. This is because it is spiritual and the spiritual is open to the spiritual and lives spiritually, through thinking and willing. So all the rational life we can observe in our bodies belongs to the soul and none of it to the body. Actually, the body is material, as just noted, and the matter that makes up the body is an added element, almost like an extension to the spirit. Its purpose is to enable our spirit to lead its life and perform its services in a physical world that is material in all respects and essentially lifeless. Since matter is not alive—only spirit is—we may conclude that whatever is alive in us is our spirit and that the body only serves it exactly the way a tool serves a living force that makes it move. We may, of course, say that a tool works or moves or strikes, but it is a mistake to believe that this is a property of the tool and not of the person who is wielding it.

Since everything that is alive in the body—everything that acts and senses things because it is alive—belongs to the spirit alone and none of it belongs to the body, it follows that the spirit is the actual person. In other words, when seen for what we really are, we are spirits, and we also have the same form as our spirits. You see, everything inside us that is alive and senses things belongs to our spirit, and there is nothing in us, from head to toe, that is not alive and able to experience the senses. This is why when our bodies are separated from our spirits, which is called dying, we still continue to be human and to be alive.

I have heard from heavenly sources that some dead people—while they are lying in the coffin, before they have been restored to life after death—continue to think even in their cold bodies. They cannot help but feel that they are alive, except that they cannot move a single atom of the matter that makes up their bodies.

We could not think or will anything if there were nothing supporting our thought and will—some substance where thinking and willing arise and in which they take place. We may imagine something happening apart from a supporting substance, but nothing like that exists. We can tell this from the fact that we could not see without an organ that supports our sight, or hear without an organ that supports our hearing. Apart from these, sight and hearing would be nothing, would not exist. The same holds true for thought, which is inner sight, and for perception, which is inner hearing. Unless these arose from and happened in substances that took the form of supporting organs, they would not happen at all. We may gather from this that our spirit is also in a form, that its form is that of a human being, and that it possesses its senses and sensory organs when it is separated from its body just as it did when it was in its body. We may gather that the entire experience of the eye, the entire experience of the ear, in fact our sensory experience as a whole belongs not to the body but to the spirit, which occupies the sensory organs completely, right through to their smallest feature.

This is why spirits see and hear and experience their senses just as much as we do, though after they have left the body this sensing does not take place in the physical world but in the spiritual one. When they were in the body, their mental experience of the senses on the physical level occurred through the material part that was an added element to their spirit. However, they were throughout that time having mental experiences purely on the spiritual level through their thinking and willing.

I have presented this to persuade rational people that, when seen for what we really are, we are spirits, and that the physical part added to us so that we can function in the physical and material world is not the real person but only the tool of our spirit.

A great deal of experience has taught me that with respect to our inner self we are spirits—experience that would fill whole volumes, as they say, if I were to include it all. I have talked with spirits as a spirit and I have talked with them as a person in a body. When I have talked with them as a spirit, they could not tell that I was not a spirit myself, in a form just as human as theirs. That is how my inner self looked to them, because when I talked with them as a spirit, they could not see my material body.

Our Life after Death

We may conclude that we are spirits with respect to our inner self from the fact that after we depart from our bodies, which happens when we die, we are still alive and just as human as ever. To convince me of this, I was allowed to talk with almost all the people I had ever met during their physical lives, with some for a few hours, with some for weeks and months, and with some for years. This was primarily so that I could be convinced and could bear witness.

I may add here that even while we are living in our bodies, each one of us is, with respect to our own spirits, in a community with other spirits even though we are unaware of it. By means of their spirits, good people are in angelic communities and evil people are in hellish communities. Furthermore, we come into those same communities when we die. People who are coming into the company of spirits after death are often told and shown this.

Actually, we are not visible as spirits in our spiritual communities while we are living in the world, because we are thinking on the physical level. However, if our thinking is directed away from our bodies we are sometimes visible in our communities because we are then in the spirit. When we are visible, it is easy to tell us from the spirits who live there because we walk along deep in thought, silent, without looking at others, as though we did not see them; and the moment any spirit speaks to us, we disappear.

To illustrate the fact that we are spirits inwardly, I would like to explain from personal experience what happens when we are taken out of the body and how we are carried away by the spirit to another place.

Inwardly We Are Spirits

The first experience, being taken out of the body, is like this. We are brought into a particular state of being that is halfway between sleep and waking. When we are in this state, it seems exactly as though we were awake; all our senses are as alert as they are when we are fully awake physically—sight, hearing, and amazingly, touch, which is then more exquisitely keen than it can ever be during physical wakefulness. This is the state in which people have seen spirits and angels most vividly, even hearing them and, strange to say, touching them, with hardly anything physical interfering. It is the state described as *being taken out of one's body and not knowing whether one is in one's body or outside it* [2 Corinthians 12:2–4].

I have been admitted to this state three or four times, simply to let me know what it was like, and also to teach me that spirits and angels have the use of all the senses and that so do we, with respect to our spirits, when we are taken out of our bodies.

As for the second kind of experience, being carried away by the spirit to another place, I have been shown by firsthand experience what happens and how it happens, but only two or three times. I should like to cite just one experience. While I was walking through city streets and through the countryside, absorbed in conversation with spirits, it seemed exactly as though I were just as awake and observant as ever, walking without getting lost, though all the while I was having visions. I was seeing woods, rivers, mansions, houses, people, and more. After I had been walking for some hours, though, I suddenly found myself back in an awareness of my physical sight and realized that I was somewhere else. I was utterly amazed by this, and realized that I had been in the state of those people who are described as *being carried away by the spirit to another place* [1 Kings 18:12; Acts 8:39–40]; for as long as it lasted I was not thinking about my route, even though it might have been many miles, or about the time, though it might have been many hours or even days. I was not conscious of any fatigue, either. This is how we can be led by routes we know nothing of, right to some predetermined place, without becoming lost.

These two states of being, though, which are states we have when we are awake to our deeper nature or (which is the same thing) to our spirit, are out of the ordinary. They were shown me simply to teach me what they were like because people in the church know of them. But talking with spirits, being with them as one of them—this is something it was granted me to do when I was fully awake physically, and it has been so for many years.

Saying that we are spirits in our inner self is the same as saying that the things that have to do with our thinking and willing are spiritual, because thinking and willing actually are our inner being. They are what make us human, and the kind of human beings we are depends on what our thinking and our willing are like.

OUR REVIVAL FROM DEATH

When someone's body can no longer perform its functions in the material world in response to the thoughts and emotions of its spirit, which come to it from the spiritual world, then we say that the individual has died. This happens when the breathing of the lungs and the pumping motion of the heart have ceased. But in fact that person has not died at all. He or she is only separated from the physicality that was useful to that individual in the world. The essential person is actually still alive. I say that because it is not our bodies that make us human, but our spirits. After all, it is the spirit inside us that thinks; and thought, along with emotion, makes us human.

We can see, then, that when we die we simply move from one world into another. This is why in the inner meaning of the Word, "death" means resurrection and a continuation of life.

Our spirits are very closely linked with our breathing and our heartbeat. Thought links to our breathing, and love's emotion links to our heart. As a result, when these two motions in the body cease, a separation immediately occurs. It is these two motions, the respiratory motion of the lungs and the pumping of the heart, that are the essential ties. Once they are severed, the spirit is left to itself; and the body, being now without the life of its spirit, cools and decays.

The reason our spirits are very closely linked with our breathing and our heart is that all our vital processes depend on these, not only in the body as a whole, but in every part as well.

After this separation, our spirit stays in the body briefly, but not after the heart has completely stopped, which occurs at different times depending on the cause of death. In some cases the motion of the heart continues for quite a while, and in others it does not. The moment it does stop, we are awakened, but only the Lord awakens us. "Being awakened" means having our spirit led out of our body and into the spiritual world. It is commonly called "resurrection."

The reason our spirit is not separated from our body until the motion of the heart has stopped is that the heart corresponds to love's emotion, which is our essential life, since all of us get our vital warmth from love. So as long as the heart and the emotions are joined, the correspondence remains, and the life of the spirit is still in the body.

I have not only been told how the awakening happens, I have been shown by firsthand experience. The actual experience happened to me so that I could have a full knowledge of how it occurs.

I was brought into a state in which my physical senses were inoperative—very much, then, like the state of people who are dying. However, my deeper life and thought remained intact so that I could perceive and retain what was happening to me and what happens to people who are being awakened from death. I noticed that my physical breathing was almost suspended, and a deeper breathing, a breathing of the spirit, continued along with a very slight and silent physical one.

At first a connection was established between my heartbeat and the heavenly kingdom, because that kingdom corresponds to the human heart. I also saw angels from that kingdom, some at a distance, but two sitting close to my head. The effect was to take away all my own emotions, but to leave me still in possession of thought and higher perception. I remained in this state for several hours.

Then the spirits who were around me gradually drew away, thinking that I was dead. I sensed a sweet odor like that of an embalmed body, because when heavenly angels are present anything having to do with a corpse smells sweet. When spirits sense this, they cannot come near. This is also how evil spirits are kept away from our spirit when we are being admitted into eternal life.

The angels who were sitting beside my head were silent, simply sharing their thoughts with mine. When the deceased accepts those thoughts, the angels know that the person's spirit is ready to be led out of the body. They accomplished this sharing of thoughts by looking into my face. This is actually how thoughts are shared in heaven.

Since I had been left in possession of thought and higher perception so that I could learn and remember how awakening happens, I noticed that at first the angels were examining my thoughts to see whether they were like those of dying individuals, who are normally thinking about eternal life. They wanted to keep my mind in these thoughts. I was later told that as the body is breathing its last, our spirit is kept in its final thought until eventually it comes back to the thoughts that flowed from our basic or ruling love in the world.

I was in particular allowed to perceive and even to feel that there was a pull, a kind of drawing out of the deeper levels of my mind and therefore of my spirit from my body; and I was told that this was being done by the Lord and that it is what brings about our resurrection.

When heavenly angels are with people who have been awakened they do not leave them, because they love everyone. But some spirits are simply unable to be in the company of heavenly angels very long and want them to leave. When this happens, angels from the Lord's spiritual kingdom arrive, through whom we are granted the use of light, since before this we could not see anything but could only think.

I was also shown how this is done. It seemed as though the angels rolled back a covering from my left eye toward the bridge of my nose so that my eye was opened and able to see. To the spirit, it seems as though this were actually happening, but it is only apparently so. As this covering seemed to be rolled back, I could see a kind of bright but diffused light like the light we see through our eyelids when we are first waking up. It seemed to me as though this bright, diffused light had a heavenly color to it, but I was later told that this varies. After that, it felt as though something were being rolled gently off my face, and once this was done I had access to spiritual thought. This rolling of something off the face is an appearance, and it represents the fact that we are moving from physical thinking to spiritual thinking. Angels take the greatest care to shield the awakening person from any concept that does not have love in it. Then they tell the individual that she or he is a spirit.

After the spiritual angels have given us the use of light, they do everything for us as newly arrived spirits that we could ever wish for in that state of being. They tell us about the realities of the other life, or at least as much about them as we can grasp. However, if we are the kind of people that do not want to be taught, then once we are awakened we want to get out of the company of angels. Still, the angels do not leave us; instead we leave them. Angels really do love everyone. They want nothing more than to help people, to teach them, to lead them into heaven. This is their highest joy.

When spirits leave the company of angels, they are welcomed by the good spirits who are accompanying them and who also do all they can for them. However, if they have led the kind of life in the world that makes it impossible for them to be in the company of good people, then they want to get away from these as well. This happens as long and as many times as necessary, until they find the company of people their earthly life has fitted them for. Here they find their life; and remarkable as it may sound, they then lead the same kind of life they once led in the world.

This first stage of our life after death does not last more than a few days, though. In the following pages I will be describing how we are then brought from one state of being into another until finally we arrive either in heaven or in hell. This too is something I have been allowed to learn from a great deal of experience.

I have talked with some people on the third day after their death, when the events previously described have been completed. I talked with three whom I had known in the world and told them that their funeral services were now being planned so that their bodies could be buried. When they heard this, they were struck with a kind of bewilderment. They said that they were alive, and that what was being buried had been useful to them only in the material world. Later on, they were quite amazed at the fact that while they had been living in their bodies they had not believed in this kind of life after death, and still more that this disbelief was shared by almost everyone in the church.

Some people during their earthly lives have not believed the soul had any life after the life of the body. When they discover that they are still alive, they are deeply embarrassed. However, people who have convinced themselves that there is no eternal life join up with others who think similarly, and they move away from people who lived in faith while on earth. Most of them link up with some hellish community because such people reject the Divine and have no use for the truths of the church. In fact, the more that we convince ourselves that the eternal life of the soul cannot be, the more we convince ourselves that nothing to do with heaven and the church is real.

AFTER DEATH, WE ARE
IN A FULLY HUMAN FORM

The fact that the form of a spirit-person is the human form follows from what has been presented earlier.

This may be grasped even more clearly from the fact that we
are human because of our spirit, not because of our body, and
because our physical form is appended to the spirit in keeping
with its form, not the other way around, since a spirit is clothed
with a body that matches its form. As a result, the human spirit
acts on the individual parts of the body, including the smallest
ones, even to the point that any part that is not activated by the
spirit, any part in which there is no spirit acting, is not alive.
Anyone can see this by considering that thought and willpower
activate absolutely everything in the body and are so completely
in control that no part of the body dissents. If anything does
not consent it is not part of the body, and it is actually expelled
as something with no life in it. Thought and will belong to the
spirit, not to the body.

The reason we cannot see the human form of the spirits who have left the body and of the spirits that are inside the people we meet is that our physical organ of sight, the eye, is material with respect to the seeing it does in this world, and what is material sees only what is material. What is spiritual, though, sees what is spiritual; so when the material eye is covered over and loses its coordination with the spirit, then spirits are visible in their own form, which is human. And it is a human form not only for the spirits who are in the spiritual world but also for the spirits in people we meet while they are still in their bodies.

The reason the form of a spirit is a human one is that in regard to our spirits we have been created in the form of heaven, since all of heaven and its design are summed up in what makes up the human mind. This is the source of our ability to take in intelligence and wisdom. (It makes no difference whether you talk about our ability to take in intelligence and wisdom or our ability to take in heaven.)

Years and years of daily experience have provided me with evidence that after separation from the body the human spirit is a person and is in a similar form. I have seen this thousands of times, I have heard such spirits, and I have even talked with them about the fact that people in the world don't believe that they are what they are. I've told them that scholars think people who do believe such things are naive.

Spirits are heartsick over the fact that this kind of ignorance is still common in the world and especially in the church. But they say that this belief is spread in particular by academics who have thought about the soul only on the basis of the bodily senses. The only conclusion these academics can come to by thinking this way is that the soul is only a concept, and since it does not exist in any medium in which and from which it can be seen, it's like pure ether, which readily evaporates, and it can only fade into nothingness when the body dies. But since the church believes in the immortality of the soul on the basis of the Word, these scholars are forced to concede that the soul has some tinge of life, something thought-ish. Despite this concession, they don't allow the soul any ability to sense things the way we do, or at least not until it's reunited with its body. Their doctrine of the resurrection is based on this idea, as is their belief that there will be a reunion of soul and body when the Last Judgment comes. The result is that when people put doctrine and speculation together and think about the soul on that basis, they just don't get the fact that the soul is the spirit and that it has a human form. To say nothing of the fact that hardly anyone nowadays knows what "spiritual" means, let alone knows that spirit-people (that is, spirits and angels) have a human form.

Thus almost all the people who arrive from this world are absolutely astounded to find that they are alive and that they are just as human as ever, that they are seeing and hearing and talking, that their bodies still possess the sense of touch, and that nothing at all has changed. But once they get over that, then they go on to be astonished that the church doesn't know anything about this state of being we have after death, and so is similarly ignorant about heaven and hell, even though all the people who have lived in this world are in the other life and are living people.

Because people there kept wondering why this has not been made plain to people on earth through visions, since it is critical to the faith of the church to know about it, they were told by a heavenly source that such visions could be granted whenever it pleased the Lord—nothing could be easier. But, they were told, even if people had such visions, no one would believe them, because they have all convinced themselves of the exact opposite.

When we first enter the world of spirits (which happens shortly after the reawakening just described), our face and the sound of our voice are the same as they were in the world. This is because at that point we are in a state of being in which we are focused on our outer self, and our inner self has not yet been revealed to us. This is our initial state after we have died. Later, though, our face changes and becomes quite different. It comes to look like the ruling love that the deeper reaches of our mind focused on in the world, the kind of love characteristic of the spirit within our body, because the face of our spirit is very different from the face of our body. We get our physical face from our parents and our spiritual face from our ruling love, of which our face forms an image. Our spirit takes on this face after our physical life is over, when the outer coverings have been removed.

I have seen some newcomers from the world and have recognized them by their faces and voices; but when I saw them later, I did not recognize them. People whose ruling love was good had beautiful faces, while people whose ruling love was evil had ugly ones. If our spirit is seen for what it really is, it is identical to our love. And our face is just the outward shape of our love.

The reason our faces change is that in the other life no one is allowed to pretend to love something they really don't, so we can't put on a face that is the opposite of the love that guides us. All of us are shifted to a state of being in which we say what we think and show what we want to do in our expressions and actions. This is why our faces take on the shape of what we love and form an image of it; and this is why all the people who have known each other in the world still recognize each other in the world of spirits, but not in heaven or hell.

The faces of hypocrites change more slowly than those of other people, because by constant practice they have formed the habit of arranging their inner selves into a counterfeit of a love for what is good. So for a long time they look fairly attractive. However, since this false front is gradually stripped off and the deeper elements of their minds are gradually arranged in the shape of what they love, they wind up uglier than other people.

Hypocrites are people who talk like angels but who inwardly respect only material things, not the Divine Being, and who therefore deny the reality of anything having to do with the church and heaven.

One thing we should be sure about is that our human form will be all that much more beautiful after death if we have deeply loved divine truths and have lived by them, since our deeper levels are opened and shaped according to both our love of these truths and the way we live. So the deeper our love and the more it is like heaven, the more beautiful our faces will be. This is why the angels who are in the very deepest heaven are the most beautiful—because they are forms of heavenly love. On the other hand, there are people who have loved divine truths more with their outer selves and for that reason have lived by them in more superficial ways, and they are less beautiful. This is because only the more superficial qualities shine from their faces; and no deeper, heavenly love can shine through those superficial qualities. And if that love doesn't shine through, then neither does the shape of what heaven really is. In their faces you can see something that is dim by comparison with heaven—something that can't come to life, because no deeper life inside is lighting it up.

To put it briefly: the deeper anything is, the closer it is to being perfect; the more superficial it is, the farther it is from being perfect. And our beauty varies depending on how close to perfection we are.

I have seen faces of angels of the third heaven so beautiful that no painters, with all their skill and pigment, could render a fraction of their light or rival a thousandth part of the radiance and vitality that show in their faces. By contrast, the faces of angels of the outermost heaven could just possibly be captured in a painting.

Finally, I should like to offer a secret never before made known: Everything good and true that comes from the Lord and makes up heaven is in the form of a human being. This is true not only of the totality of heaven, on a grand scale, but also of each individual part of heaven, on the smallest scale. This heavenly form has an effect on everyone who takes in what is good and what is true from the Lord: the more those in heaven take in these things, the more truly human in form they are. This is why heaven is self-consistent throughout, both in what is shared by all and in its individual parts. It is also why the human form is the form of the whole of heaven, and of each community, and of each angel. And, it should be added, this is why the human form is the form taken even by the individual thoughts born from the heavenly love found among angels.

This secret may not make sense to anyone on earth, but it makes perfect sense to angels, because they stand in heaven's light.

WE LEAVE NOTHING BEHIND
EXCEPT OUR EARTHLY BODY

Repeated experience has proved to me that when we move from the material world into the spiritual, which happens when we die, we take with us everything that pertains to our character except our earthly body. In fact, when we enter the spiritual world, or our life after death, we are in a body as we were in this world. Since we don't feel or see any difference, it seems as if nothing has changed. Now our body is spiritual, though, which means it has been separated from earthly matter and purified. Furthermore, when anything spiritual touches and sees something spiritual, it is just like something material touching and seeing something material. So when we have become a spirit, none of our senses tells us that we are not in the body we inhabited in the world, and therefore we do not realize that we have died.

As spirit-people, we possess every outer and inner sense we had in the world. We see the way we used to, we hear and talk the way we used to; we smell and taste; we feel it when we are touched just the way we used to; we want, wish, crave, think, ponder, are moved, love, and intend the way we used to. Studious types still read and write the way they did before. In a word, when we move from the one life into the other, or from the one world into the other, it is like moving from one physical place to another; and we take with us everything we possessed as human beings, to the point that it would be untrue to say that we have lost anything of our own after death, which is only a death of the earthly body. We even take with us our earthly memory, since we retain everything we have heard, seen, read, learned, or thought in the world from earliest infancy to the very end of life. But since the earthly objects that reside in our memory are beyond our power to retrieve in a world that is spiritual, they become dormant there the way they do when we are not thinking about them. They can, however, be retrieved when it so pleases the Lord. But I will have more to say soon about the earthly memory and its condition after death.

People who are focused on their senses are quite incapable of believing that our state after death is like this, because they can't conceive of such a thing. Such people can think only on the material level, even about spiritual matters. This means that anything they do not sense—that is, anything they do not see with their physical eyes and touch with their hands—they say does not exist, as we read of Thomas in John 20:25, 27, 29.

Nevertheless, the difference between our life in the spiritual world and our life in the material world is considerable, with respect both to our outer senses and the way they affect us, and to our inner senses and the way they affect us. People who are in heaven are far more sensitive mentally. That is, they see and hear and also think more discerningly than when they were in this world. This is because they are seeing in heaven's light, which vastly surpasses the world's light, and they hear by way of a spiritual atmosphere that vastly surpasses the atmosphere of the earth. The difference this makes to their outer senses is as great as the difference we see in the material world between clear skies and the obscurity of a cloud, or between noonday light and the dimness of evening. Because the light of heaven is divine truth, it enables angels to notice and distinguish between even the smallest things by sight. Furthermore, their outer sight corresponds to their inner sight (their understanding), since for angels each sight flows into the other and they act as a single faculty. This is why both the outer sight of angels and their inner vision are so sharp. Their hearing corresponds in a similar way to their higher perception, which is a function of both their understanding and their will. So in the tone and words of others, angels pick up the slightest shadings of the speakers' emotion and thought—shadings of emotion in the tone, and shadings of thought in the words.

However, angels' other senses are not as exquisitely keen as their sight and hearing, because sight and hearing serve their intelligence and wisdom, while the other senses do not. If the others were as sharp, they would take away the illumination and the joy that angels find in wisdom and replace them with a joy in pleasures arising from physical appetites that obscure and weaken the intellect more and more as they become stronger. This happens to people in the world as well, who become more dull and mindless with respect to spiritual truths the more they indulge their appetite for food and yield to the body's yearning for the gratification of physical touch.

The deeper senses of heaven's angels, which are connected with their thought and emotion, are more exquisitely keen and more close to perfection than the ones they had in the world.

As for our keeping our complete memory when we leave the world, I have been shown this by many examples and have seen and heard a great deal worth mentioning. I would like to list a few examples.

There were people who denied the crimes and transgressions they had committed in the world. To prevent them from being seen as blameless, everything was revealed and drawn out of their own memory in chronological order from the beginning of their life to the end. Most of these transgressions were acts of adultery and fornication.

There were people who had deceived others with malicious skill and had stolen from them. Their deceptions and thefts were also recounted one after the other, many of which were known to practically no one in the world other than themselves. They admitted them, too, because they were plain as day, along with all the thoughts, intentions, pleasures, and fears that were swirling together in their minds at the time.

There were people who had taken bribes and made money from judicial decisions. They were similarly examined on the basis of their own memories, and everything was recounted from their first taking office to the end. Hundreds upon hundreds of details of how much they took, and what kinds of things, at what time, and their mental state and their intentions, were all simultaneously recalled to their remembrance and exposed to view. In some cases, remarkably enough, the very ledgers in which they had recorded these actions were opened and read to them, page by page.

There were men who had seduced innocent women in order to corrupt them and violate them. They were summoned to a similar judgment, and the details were drawn out of their memory and listed. The actual faces of the young women and others were presented as though they were there in person, along with where the men took them, what the men told them, what they were thinking. It was done as instantaneously as when something is actually being witnessed firsthand. Sometimes these presentations lasted for hours.

There was one man who thought nothing of speaking ill of other people. I heard his slanders recounted in chronological order, and his false testimony against them too—the actual words, and which individual he was slandering, and who was present. All these details were brought out and presented in one stroke as if they were real life, though he had very carefully kept them hidden while he was living in the world.

There was one man who had defrauded a relative of his legacy by some devious pretext. He was convicted and sentenced in the same way. Remarkably, the letters and documents they exchanged were read aloud to me, and he said that not a word was missing. This same man had also secretly killed a neighbor by poison just before his own death, a fact that was disclosed in the following way. He appeared to be digging a trench under his feet, and when it had been dug, a man came out as though from a tomb and shouted at him, "What have you done to me?" Then everything was revealed—how the poisoner had talked in a friendly way with him and offered him the drink, what he had thought beforehand, and what happened afterward. Once this was uncovered, the murderer was condemned to hell.

In a word, all the evils, crimes, thefts, frauds, and deceptions committed by evil spirits are made clear to them and drawn directly from their own memories, and they are convicted. They cannot possibly deny anything, because all the circumstances are presented together.

I also heard that angels have seen and displayed from the memory of one individual everything he had thought, one day after another, over the course of a month, with not one single mistake. These memories were recalled to him as though he himself were back in those very days.

We may gather from these instances that we take our complete memory with us, and that nothing is so concealed in this world that it will not be made known after death, and made known in public, according to the Lord's words: "Nothing is hidden that will not be revealed, and nothing concealed that will not become known. Whatever you have said in the dark will be heard in the light, and what you have spoken in someone's ear will be proclaimed on the rooftops" (Luke 12:2–3).

When we are being confronted after death with what we have done in life, angels who have been given the task of examining us look searchingly in our faces and continue their examination through our entire bodies, beginning with the fingers first of one hand and then of the other, and continuing through everything else. When I wondered why this was so, it was explained to me. The reason is that just as the details of our thought and will are inscribed on the brain, because that is where their physical beginnings are, they are also inscribed on the whole body, since whatever arises from our thought and our will moves from the point where it begins out into the body and is realized there in its final form. This is why the things that are inscribed on our memory that come from our will, and from the thought that arises from our willing something, are inscribed not only on the brain but also on the whole person, where they take form in a pattern that follows the pattern of the parts of the body. I could therefore see that our overall character depends on the kinds of things we will to do, and on the thoughts that we have as a result. In fact, it can be said that evil people *are* their own evil and good people *are* their own good.

We can also gather from this what is meant by our book of life, which is mentioned in the Word. Specifically, the meaning is that all our actions and all our thoughts are written on our whole person and seem as though they are read from a book when they are called out of our memory. They appear as a kind of image when our spirit is looked at in heaven's light.

I would like to add to this something noteworthy about the memory that we keep after death, something that convinced me that not just the general contents but even the smallest details that have entered our memory do last and are never erased. I saw some books with writing in them like earthly writing, and I was told that they had come *from the memories* of the people who had originally written them—that not a single word was missing that had been in the books written by those people in the material world. I was also told that in the same way, the tiniest details about everything could be retrieved from the memory of another person, even things that individual had forgotten while on earth. The reason for this was explained as well: namely, that we have an outer and an inner memory. The outer belongs to our material person and the inner belongs to our spiritual person. The details of what we have thought, willed, said, and done, even what we have heard and seen, are inscribed on our inner or spiritual memory. There is no way to erase anything there, since everything is written at once on our spirit itself and on the parts of our body, as has been mentioned. This means that our spirit is formed in accordance with what we have thought and what we have willed to do. I know that these things seem contrary to reason, and thus hard to believe, but they are true nevertheless.

So never believe that there is anything we have thought or done in secret that will remain hidden after death. Believe instead that absolutely everything will come out into the light of day.

Although our outer or material memory is still part of us after death, when we reach the other life we cannot remember anything that is merely material. We can retrieve from our memory only spiritual things that are connected to the material ones by correspondences. Still, when those correspondences are presented visually, they look just as they did in the material world. This is because everything we see in the heavens looks as it did in the world, even though in essence it is not material but spiritual.

As for our outer or material memory, though, inasmuch as its contents are derived from matter, time, space, and everything else that characterizes the material world, it does not serve the same function for the spirit that it served in the world. This is because in the world, when we based our thinking on our outer senses and not at the same time on our inner senses—the senses that belong to our higher understanding—we were thinking on the material level and not on the spiritual one. However, in the other life, when our spirit is in the spiritual world, we do not think on the material level but on the spiritual one. Thinking on the spiritual level is thinking with our higher understanding, our reasoning powers. This is why our outer or material memory then goes dormant as far as material things are concerned. The only things our memory uses are what we have gained in the world through those material things and have made a part of our reasoning ability.

This is why we possess the ability to reason after death to the extent that we have acquired that ability through our use of languages and the arts and sciences in this world, and emphatically not to the extent that we have just gained knowledge about languages and arts and sciences. I have talked with any number of people who were regarded as learned in the world because of their knowledge of such ancient languages as Hebrew and Greek and Latin, but who had not developed their ability to reason by means of the things that were written in those languages. Some of them seemed as simple as people who did not know anything about those languages; some of them seemed dense, but still they were full of conceit, as though they were wiser than other people.

I have talked with some people who had written a great deal when they were in the world, some of them in all kinds of academic fields, people who had therefore gained an international reputation for learning. Some of them could quibble about whether truths were true or not. Some of them understood what was true when they turned toward people who were in the light of truth; but since they still did not want to understand what was true, they denied it when they were focused on their own false opinions and were therefore really being themselves. Some of them did not know any more than the illiterate masses. So they varied depending on the way they had developed their reasoning ability through the treatises they had written or copied. Still, if they had opposed the truths of the church, had based their thinking on academic disciplines, and had used them to convince themselves of false principles, they had not developed their reasoning ability but only their skill in argumentation—an ability that is confused with reasoning in the world, but is in fact a different ability. It is an ability to prove anything one pleases, to see what is false rather than what is true, all on the basis of preconceptions and illusions. People like this can never be brought to recognize truths, because it is impossible to see truths on the basis of false principles—though on the basis of true principles it is possible to see what is false.

Our reasoning ability is like a garden or flower bed, like newly tilled land. Our memory is the soil, information and knowledge gained from experience are the seeds, and heaven's light and warmth make them productive. There is no germination without the last two. So there is no germination in us unless heaven's light, which is divine truth, and heaven's warmth, which is divine love, are allowed in. They are the only source of our ability to reason.

Angels are profoundly grieved that scholars have, for the most part, continued to identify nature as the cause of all things, and have therefore closed the deeper levels of their minds until they can see no trace of truth from the light of truth, which is the light of heaven. As a result, in the other life scholars are actually deprived of their ability to reason, so that they will not use reason to spread false notions among simple and good people and mislead them. They are banished to deserted areas.

One particular spirit resented the fact that he could not remember much of what he had known during his physical life. He was grieving over the pleasure he had lost, because what he had memorized had been his main source of enjoyment. He was told, though, that he had not lost anything at all and that he knew absolutely everything he had known before. It was just that in the world where he was now living, he was not allowed to retrieve things of that kind from his memory. It should satisfy him that his thought and speech were far better, more nearly perfect, and that now he did not smother his power to reason with the dense darkness of material trivia the way he had before, in concerns that were useless in the kingdom he had now reached. Now he had all he needed to live eternally, and it was by using that and nothing else that he could become blessed and happy. So it was pure ignorance to believe that his intelligence had died out just because in this kingdom the facts of the material world had been set to one side and had gone dormant in his memory.

The truth of the matter, he was told, is that the more the mind can be guided out of what belongs to the senses of the outer self and the body, the more it is raised toward what is spiritual and heavenly.

Sometimes in the other life a demonstration is made to show what the two kinds of memories are like, and they are given visible shape, though the shapes are only appearances there. (In that world many things are presented visually that for us here remain purely in the realm of ideas.) In these demonstrations, the outer memory is shown as a callus, while the inner looks like the medullary substance found in the human brain.

This appearance also helps us understand what these two kinds of memory are like. In people who have focused solely on memorizing knowledge during their physical lives, without developing their powers of reasoning, the memory has a callused quality that looks hard and streaked with tendons inside. In people who have filled their memories with false notions, it looks shaggy and hairy because of the random mass of disorganized stuff it contains. In people who have eagerly memorized knowledge, keeping themselves and the world uppermost in their minds, it looks stuck-together and bony. In people who have tried to use acquired facts, especially facts about philosophy, to learn secrets about the Divine, without actually believing in anything unless they are first convinced by those acquired facts—in such people the memory looks dark, and it can actually absorb rays of light and turn those rays into darkness. In people who have been deceitful and hypocritical, the memory looks bony and hard as ivory, and it repels rays of light.

However, in people who have focused on the good that we do out of love and on the truths that we know because of faith, no such callus is visible. This is because their inner memory is beaming rays of light into their outer memory, and those rays come to rest in the contents or concepts of the outer memory, and are intensely satisfied in finding something to contain them there (it is as though those concepts were their foundation or the ground beneath them). In the divine design the outer memory is the very outermost layer, where spiritual and heavenly matters gently fill out their outline and remain firm, as long as there are good and true contents in it.

While we are living in the world, if we are engaged in a love for the Lord and in loving behavior toward our neighbor, we have angelic intelligence and wisdom with us and even inside us, but it is hidden away in the depths of our inner memory and cannot become visible until we leave our bodies. Then our material memory is put to sleep, and we are awakened into an awareness of our inner memory and eventually of our actual angelic memory.

Spirits and angels have memory just as we do. What they hear and see and think and intend and do stays with them; and through their memory they are constantly developing their ability to reason. This process goes on forever. This is why spirits and angels are being perfected in intelligence and wisdom through experiences of what is true and good, just the way we are.

The fact that spirits and angels have the ability to remember is yet another thing I have been shown by a great deal of experience. I have seen everything they had thought and done, both in public and in private, called up from their memory when they were with other spirits. I have also seen people who, because of a simple goodness in themselves, had been focused on some truth; and once they have been filled with insights, and with the intelligence that developed from those insights, they are taken up into heaven.

It's important for us to realize, though, that these people are not filled with insights, and with the understanding that comes from insights, beyond the level of the affection for what is good and true that they had reached in the world. In fact, each spirit and angel retains the amount and kind of affection he or she had in the world, and this is afterward perfected by being filled in with more. This filling in goes on forever, since everything is capable of infinite variation and enrichment by different means, so that it can be multiplied and can bear fruit. There is no end to any instance of goodness, since its source is the Infinite.

WHAT WE ARE LIKE AFTER DEATH

Any Christian knows from the Word that our life continues after death. It says in many places that we will be judged and rewarded according to our actions. Furthermore, people who use goodness and real truth to do their thinking cannot help but see that those who lead good lives enter heaven and those who lead evil lives enter hell. However, people who are intent on evil do not want to believe that their state after death depends on their life in the world. They think rather—and especially when their health begins to fail—that heaven is granted to all people purely through God's mercy, no matter how they may have lived. They think that gaining heaven requires only faith, which they consider to have nothing to do with the way one lives.

Though it does say in many places in the Word that we will be judged for our actions and rewarded accordingly, "actions" in the Word does not refer only to the way actions appear outwardly. It also refers to what actions really are inside. Everyone knows, of course, that all our actions come from our will and our thought. If they didn't come from our willing and thinking, they would

43

be no better than the kind of motions that machines or robots make. So actions, if you look at them for what they really are, are just the realizations of our will and thought. They get their soul and life from our will and thought; they *are* our will and thought in an outward form.

So we know that the quality of our actions is determined by the will and thought they result from. If our will and thought are good, then our actions are good; but if our will and thought are evil, then our actions are evil, even though they may look the same on the outside. A thousand people can do the same thing—that is, they can each do something that is so much like what the others are doing that from the outward appearance you can hardly tell the difference—but each action, if you look at what it really is, *does* differ from the others, because it results from a different intention.

Take, for example, behaving honestly and fairly toward someone you know. One person can behave honestly and fairly toward someone else in order to seem honest and fair for the sake of his or her own self, and to gain respect; another person can do the same for the sake of worldly profit; a third person to be rewarded and get credit for being good; a fourth to win friends; a fifth out of fear of getting into trouble with the law or of losing a good reputation or a job; a sixth to enlist people in some cause, even an evil cause; a seventh in order to mislead people; and others for still other reasons. But even though what they do looks good (and behaving honestly and fairly toward someone you know certainly is good), still their actions are evil because they don't do them because they love honesty and fairness for the sake of honesty and fairness. They do them because they love themselves and material things, for the sake of themselves and material things. Honesty and fairness just serve what they really love, like hired servants. When those servants are of no use to their employer, they are viewed as worthless and are sent away.

When people behave honestly and fairly toward someone they know, and they really are acting from a love for what is honest and fair, the outward form of what they do looks just the same as when others do it, [but again, it can be done for a variety of reasons]. Some of these people act that way because of the truth of what they believe, or out of obedience, because the Word makes being honest and fair into a key principle. Some of them act that way because of the goodness of what they believe, or out of conscience, because they are moved by religious feeling. Some of them act that way because it is good to be kind toward one's neighbor and because taking thought for the neighbor's welfare is important. Some of them do it out of the goodness of their love for the Lord, because what is good should be done for its own sake; so too what is honest and fair should be done for the sake of honesty and fairness. These people love these good things because they come from the Lord, and because honesty and fairness have inside them something divine that comes from the Lord. So honesty and fairness *are* divine, if we see them in their true essence. The actions of people like this are inwardly good, so their actions are outwardly good as well. As already pointed out, whether actions are bad or good is entirely determined by the thought and intention they come from, and without thought and intention they are not actions at all, only lifeless motions.

We can understand from this discussion of actions what is meant in the Word by the term *works*.

It is important to recognize that it is our will that makes us who we are. Thought contributes only to the extent that our thoughts come from our will.

Actions, then, come from both our thought and our will.

Or in other words: *love* is what makes us who we are; *faith* makes us who we are only to the extent that it comes from love; and actions come from both love and faith.

It follows from this that our will or love is who we really are, because the things that come from a person are that person's. ("To come from" means to be produced and presented in a form that can be perceived and seen.)

From this we can conclude what faith without love really is—it is no faith at all, only information with no spiritual life in it. The same holds true for actions without love. They are not living actions at all, only dead works that contain an appearance of life, which comes from a love of evil and a faith in what is false. This appearance of life is what we call spiritual death.

We should realize as well that we make our whole being visible in our actions. Our will and thought, or the love and faith that make up our inner being, are not complete until they enter into the actions that make up our outer being. Our actions are in fact the final forms that our love and faith end up in. If our will and thought do not come to their final form in our actions, they are like things that haven't been finalized and don't yet have any real presence, and so they are like things that are not yet in us at all.

To think and will to do something without acting when we can is like a flame sealed in a jar and stifled, or it is like a seed sown in the sand that does not grow but dies along with its power to reproduce. Thinking and willing and *doing*, though, is like a flame that sheds its light and warmth all around, or like a seed sown in the soil, that grows into a tree or a flower and *becomes* something. Anyone can see that willing and not acting when we can is not really willing at all, and loving and not doing good when we can is not really loving. Instead it is nothing more than thinking that we want to do something, thinking that we love; so it is just an isolated thought that melts away and vanishes.

Love and will are the very soul of actions. That soul forms a body for itself in the honest and fair things that we do. This is the only source of our spiritual body, the body of the human spirit; that is, our spiritual body is formed entirely from what we have done out of love or intent. To put it simply, our entire character and spirit are embodied in our actions.

We can see from this what is meant by the life that stays with us after death. It truly is our love and the faith that comes from our love. It is not just what our love and faith might be, but what they actually get done. So it is our actions, because these contain within themselves our whole love and faith.

There is one ruling love that remains with each of us after death and never changes to eternity. Each of us has many "loves," but they all depend on our ruling love and form a single whole with it, or when taken together they add up to it. All the parts of our will that agree with our ruling love are called "loves," because we love them. Some loves are deep and others are more superficial; some loves are directly linked together and other loves are indirectly linked together; some are near to us and others are more distant; and there are loves that are there to serve other loves in various ways. Taken all together they make a kind of kingdom. They are actually arranged in this way within us even though we are utterly unaware of their arrangement. However, the arrangement becomes visible to some extent in the other life, because the way our thoughts and emotions extend outward there depends on it. They extend outward into heavenly communities if our ruling love is made up of loves of heaven, but they extend outward into hellish communities if our ruling love is made up of loves of hell.

In the arguments I have presented so far, I have appealed only to our powers of abstract reasoning. In order to show that the topic is something we can perceive with our senses, I would like to add some experiences that may serve to illustrate and support the claims that (1) we are our love or will after death; (2) we remain the same forever with respect to our will or ruling love; (3) we go to heaven if we love heavenly and spiritual things, but we go to hell if our love is materialistic and worldly and has no heavenly and spiritual dimension; (4) our faith does not stay with us unless it comes from a heavenly love; and (5) only what our love has really done—that is, how we have lived—remains with us when we go to the next world.

A great deal of my experience has given evidence of the fact that (1) *we are our love or will after death*. All heaven is divided up into communities that love different things, and every spirit who is raised up into heaven and becomes an angel is taken to the community that loves the same thing she or he does. When we arrive there we feel as though we are in our own element—at home, back in our birthplace, so to speak. Angels sense this and associate there with spirits who are like them. When they leave and go somewhere else, they feel a constant pull, a longing to go back to their kindred spirits and therefore to their ruling love. This is how people gather together in heaven. The same applies in hell. There people associate with others according to loves that are the opposites of heavenly ones.

We can also see that we are our love after death from the fact that anything that does not agree with our ruling love is then set to one side and, to all appearances, taken away from us. For good people, what is set aside and apparently taken away is everything that disagrees and conflicts with their love, with the result that they are made to enter fully into their love. It is much the same for evil people, except that everything true is taken away from them. Either way, the result is that ultimately everyone turns into whatever love is most his or her own. This happens when we are brought into our third state, which will be discussed below.

Once this has happened, we constantly hold our faces toward our love and have it constantly before our eyes no matter which way we turn.

All spirits can be led wherever you want as long as they are kept focused on their ruling love. They cannot resist even though they know what is happening and think that they will refuse. Spirits have often tried to act in opposition to this, but without success. Their love is like a knot or rope tied around them, with which they can be pulled and which they cannot escape. It is the same for people in this world. Our love leads us as well, and it is through our love that we are led by others. It is even more so when we become spirits, though, because then we are not allowed to look as though we have a different love or to claim that a love is ours when it isn't.

It is obvious in every gathering in the other life that our spirit is our ruling love. To the extent that we act and talk in a way that agrees with a person's love, that individual looks complete, and we can see his or her whole face, which is cheerful and lively. To the extent that we act and talk in a way that disagrees with someone's ruling love, though, that individual's face begins to change, to grow dim, and to become hard to see. Eventually it disappears, as though it were not even there. I have often been amazed at this because this kind of thing cannot happen in the world. However, I have been told that the same thing happens to the spirit inside us: when we turn our attention away from other people, our spirit ceases to be perceived by theirs.

Another fact that has shown me that our spirit is our ruling love is that we eagerly take up and make our own whatever is appropriate for our love, and we reject and push away whatever is not appropriate for it. Our love is like a spongy, porous wood that absorbs whatever liquids assist its growth, but repels others. It is like animals of various kinds: they recognize their proper foods, seek out the ones that suit their natures, and avoid the ones that disagree. Every love actually wants to be nourished by what is appropriate to it—an evil love by falsity and a good love by truth. I have occasionally been allowed to see some simple and good people who wanted to teach evil people about things that were true and good. Faced with this teaching, though, the evil people fled far away; and when they reached their own kind, they seized with great pleasure on falsities that fit in with their love. I have also been allowed to see good spirits talking with each other about truths, which other good spirits in attendance listened to eagerly, while some evil spirits who were there paid no attention, as though they did not hear anything.

Paths appear in the world of spirits, some leading to heaven and some leading to hell, each one going to some specific community. Good spirits travel only the paths that lead to heaven and to the community engaged in doing the good that arises from their own particular love. They do not see paths that lead anywhere else. On the other hand, evil spirits travel only the paths that lead to hell and to the community there that is engaged in the evil that arises from their own particular love. They do not see paths that lead anywhere else; or if they do see them, in any case they do not want to follow them.

Paths like this in the spiritual world are [spiritual] realities made visible. They correspond to various things either true or false; so this is what paths in the Word symbolize.

These proofs from experience support what was said above as an appeal to reason: after death we are our own love and our own will. I say "will" because for each of us, our will is our love.

A great deal of experience has also convinced me that (2) *after death we remain the same forever with respect to our will or ruling love.* I have been allowed to talk with some people who lived more than two thousand years ago, people whose lives are described in history books and are therefore familiar. I discovered that they were still the same, just as described, and that means they were the same with respect to the love that gave rise to and determined the way they lived.

There were others who had lived seventeen centuries ago, also known from history books, and some who had lived four centuries ago, some three, and so on, with whom I was also allowed to talk and to learn that the same love still ruled them. The only difference was that the things in which their ruling love took pleasure had been exchanged for the [spiritual] pleasures that corresponded to them.

Angels have told me that the life of our ruling love never changes for anyone to all eternity because we are our love, so to change it in any spirit would be to take away and snuff out his or her life.

They have also told me that this is because after death we can no longer be reformed by being taught the way we could in this world, since the outer self, which is made up of insights and emotions arising from the material world, then goes dormant. It cannot be made active again because it is not spiritual. Our deeper mind or character is based on this outer level the way a house rests on its foundation, which is why we remain forever in the kind of life we lived as a result of our love when we were in the world.

Angels are utterly amazed that people do not realize that our ruling love determines who we are. It amazes them too that many people actually believe they can be saved by direct mercy, simply on the basis of their faith alone, regardless of the kind of life they have led, since these people do not realize that divine mercy operates indirectly. It consists of being led by the Lord in the world as well as afterward in heaven, and the people who are led by mercy are the ones who do not live in evil. People do not even know that faith is an affection for what is true, an affection that comes from a heavenly love, which in turn comes from the Lord.

(3) *We go to heaven if our love is heavenly and spiritual, and to hell if our love is materialistic and worldly and has no heavenly and spiritual dimension.* My evidence for this conclusion is all the people I have seen raised into heaven and cast into hell. The ones who were raised into heaven had lives of heavenly and spiritual love, while the ones who were cast into hell had lives of materialistic and worldly love.

Heavenly love is loving what is good, honest, and fair because it is good, honest, and fair, and doing it because of that love. This is why angels have a life of goodness, honesty, and fairness, which is a heavenly life. If we love these things for their own sakes and do or live them, we are also loving the Lord above all, because they come from him. We are also loving our neighbor, because these things are our neighbor who is to be loved.

Materialistic love, by contrast, is loving what is good and honest and fair not for its own sake but for our own purposes, because we can use them to gain fame, prestige, and profit. In this case we are not focusing on the Lord and our neighbor within what is good and honest and fair but on ourselves and the world, and we find enjoyment in deceiving people. When our motive is deceit, then whatever is good and honest and fair is actually evil and dishonest and unfair. This is what we really love within the appearance of what is good and honest and fair.

Since these loves define our lives, after we arrive in the world of spirits immediately after death we are all examined so that it can be discovered what kind of people we are. Then we are linked up with people that have a similar love. If we are focused on heavenly love, we are linked up with people in heaven; and if we are focused on materialistic love, we are linked up with people in hell. Furthermore, once the first and second states have been completed, these two kinds of people are separated so that they no longer see or recognize each other. We actually become our own love not only with respect to the deeper levels of our minds but outwardly as well, in face, body, and speech, since we become images of our love even in outer respects. People who are materialistic loves look coarse, dim, dark, and misshapen; people who are heavenly loves look lively, clear, bright, and attractive. These two kinds of people are completely different in spirit and in thought as well. People who are heavenly loves are intelligent and wise, while people who are materialistic loves are dense and rather foolish.

When one is allowed to examine the inner and outer aspects of the thoughts and affections of people engaged in heavenly love, the inner aspects look as though they were made of light, in some cases like the light of a flame; and their outer aspects are of various beautiful colors, like a rainbow. By contrast, the inner aspects of people who are engaged in materialistic love look gloomy because they are closed in, and like a smoky fire in the case of some of those whose inner selves indulged in malicious deceptions. Their outer aspects have an ugly color, depressing to look at. (Both the inner and outer aspects of the mind and spirit are presented visually in the spiritual world whenever it so pleases the Lord.)

People who are engaged in materialistic love do not see anything in heaven's light. Heaven's light is darkness to them, while hell's light, which is like the light of glowing embers, is like daylight to them. In fact, in heaven's light their inner sight is so deprived of light that they become insane. As a result, they run away from that light and hide in caves and caverns; and the more false the convictions are that arise from their evil intentions, the deeper they go. Exactly the reverse is true for people who are engaged in heavenly love, though. The deeper (or higher) they go into heavenly light, the more clearly they see everything and the more beautiful it all looks, and the more intelligently and wisely they grasp what is true.

There is no way that people who are engaged in materialistic love can live in heaven's warmth, because heaven's warmth is heavenly love. They can live in hell's warmth, though, which is a love of cruelty toward people who do not support them. This love takes pleasure in contempt for others, hostility, hatred, and vengefulness. When such people are absorbed in these pleasures, they feel truly alive, and they have no idea whatsoever what it means to do good for others out of sheer goodness, for the sake of good itself. They only know how to do good if it is done for evil reasons and for the sake of evil.

Nor can people who are engaged in materialistic love breathe when they are in heaven. When evil spirits are taken there, they breathe like people gasping in agony. On the other hand, people who are engaged in heavenly love breathe more freely and feel more alive the deeper into heaven they go.

We may gather from this that a heavenly and spiritual love is heaven for us because that love has every mark of something heavenly; and we can see, too, that materialistic and worldly love that is without any heavenly and spiritual love is hell for us because that love has every mark of something hellish.

It is clear, then, that people come into heaven who have a heavenly and spiritual love, and people come into hell who have a materialistic and worldly love without a heavenly and spiritual one.

The fact that (4) *our faith does not stay with us unless it comes from a heavenly love* has been brought home to me by so much experience that if I were to relate what I have seen and heard about it, it would fill a book all by itself. I can attest to this: there is no faith whatever, and there can be none, in people who are immersed in love of material and worldly things and are completely without any heavenly and spiritual love. Their faith consists of mere facts they have memorized. It is a secondhand belief that something is true, in which they believe only because to do so serves the purposes of their own love.

Let me add this: A number of people who merely thought they had had faith were introduced to people who really did. Once they began talking to one another, the former realized that in fact they had no faith at all. They even admitted later that simply *believing* the truth or the Word is not faith; faith is *loving* what is true from a heavenly love, and intending and doing it from a deep affection for it. I was also shown that the second-hand belief those people called faith was at best like the light of winter: because that light has no warmth, everything on earth lies motionless under the snow, locked in ice. Because their love is this way, the moment it is touched by rays of heaven's light, the light of their secondhand faith is not only extinguished but actually becomes a dense darkness in which people cannot even see themselves. At the same time, too, their deeper selves are so darkened that they cannot understand anything. Ultimately their false beliefs drive them mad.

This is the reason that all the truths such people have learned from the Word and from the teaching of the church are taken away from them—all the things they claimed were part of their faith. Instead they are filled with the false concepts that match the evil way they live. Every last one of them is made to enter fully into what he or she loves and into the false ideas that support it. Then, since truths contradict the false and evil ideas they are absorbed in, they hate the truth, they turn away from it, they reject it.

From my many experiences of what happens in heaven and in hell, I can bear witness that people who have confessed faith alone as a matter of doctrine and have lived evil lives are all in hell. I have seen thousands of them sent there.

The fact that (5) *only what our love has really done—that is, how we have lived—remains with us when we go to the next world* follows logically from what I have presented from experience and what I have just said about actions. Our actions are in fact our love actually taking place.

57

It is important that we realize that all our actions are part of our moral and civic life and for that reason they are concerned with what is honest and right and what is fair and evenhanded. What is honest and right is a matter of moral life, and what is fair and evenhanded is a matter of civic life. The love these come from is either heavenly or hellish. The actions of our moral and civic life are heavenly if we do them out of a love that is heavenly, because anything that we do out of a love that is heavenly we do because we are moved by the Lord, and everything we do because we are moved by the Lord is good. On the other hand, the actions of our moral and civic life are hellish if we do them out of a love that is hellish, since whatever we do out of this love, which is a love for ourselves and the world, we are moved to do by our own selves, and whatever we do on that basis is intrinsically evil. In fact, if we are seen for what we really are, or in terms of what our selves are, we are nothing but evil.

OUR FIRST STATE AFTER DEATH

There are three states of being that we pass through after death and before we arrive in either heaven or hell. In the first state we focus on our outer self, in the second we focus on our inner self, and in the third we focus on our preparation. The world of spirits is where we go through these states of being.

That said, some people don't go through these states at all, but are either raised into heaven or cast into hell immediately after their death. The people immediately raised into heaven are ones who were regenerated—whose regeneration prepared them for heaven—while they were in this world. People who have been prepared in this way only have to cast off the stain of their material being as they shed their bodies, and angels immediately take them into heaven. I have seen people raised up to heaven an hour after their death.

On the other hand, people whose inner character is malicious but whose outer appearance is virtuous—people who fed their malice on fraud to the bursting, and who used goodness as no more than a tool to deceive others—they are cast directly into hell. I have seen this happen to people. One of the most deceitful went head first. For others there were other ways of falling.

There are also people who are sent off into caves right after their death and in this way are segregated from people in the world of spirits. They are alternately brought out and sent back in. These are people who have treated their neighbors maliciously while pretending to behave civilly toward them.

The very good and very evil people are few, though, compared to the number of people who are kept in the world of spirits and prepared there for either heaven or hell, according to the divine plan.

We arrive in our first state of being—the state in which we focus on our outer self—immediately after our death. Everyone has an outer spiritual self and an inner spiritual self. We use the outer aspects of our spirit to adjust our physical person in the world—especially our faces, speech, and behavior—in order to interact with other people. The inner aspects of our spirit, by contrast, belong to our desire to do things and the thoughts we think as a result. They rarely show in our faces, speech, or behavior. We are trained from infancy to present ourselves as friendly, benevolent, and honest, and to conceal the thoughts that our private intentions give rise to. So we become accustomed to living in a way that is outwardly moral and civil no matter what we are like inside. As a result of this habitual behavior, we scarcely know our own inner selves, and in any case pay no attention to them.

Our first state of being after death is like our state in this world, since we are then similarly focused on our outer self. We have similar faces, voices, and characters; we lead similar moral and civic lives. This is why it still seems to us as though we were in this world unless we notice things that are out of the ordinary and remember that angels told us we were spirits when we were awakened. So the one life carries on into the other, and death is only a passage.

Since this is what we are like as spirits immediately after our life in the world, our friends and people we have known in the world then recognize us. Spirits perceive who we are, not only from our faces and voices but also from the aura of our life when they come near. In the other life, whenever we think about someone, we call up that individual's face in our thought along with many details about her or his life; and when we do this, the other is present as though called to us. Things like this happen in the spiritual world because thoughts are shared there and because space is not what it is in the material world. This is why as soon as we arrive in the other life, we are all recognized by our friends and relatives and by people we have known in one way or another, and why we talk with others and meet with them as we did during our friendship with them in the world. I have heard many times how people newly arrived from the world rejoiced to see their friends again, and how their friends rejoiced in turn that the others had come to them.

It often happens that married partners meet and exchange greetings joyfully. They stay together as well, but for a longer or shorter time depending on how happily they had lived together in the world. Ultimately, unless they had been united by true marriage love (which happens when heavenly love unites two minds), they separate after having been together for a while.

If the minds of the partners disagreed, however, and if their inner selves were repellent to each other, they break out into open hostility and sometimes actually fight with each other. Still, they are not separated until they enter the second state of being, which will be described shortly.

Since the life of newly arrived spirits is not unlike their life in the world, and since they do not know anything about life after death, or about heaven or hell, except what they have learned from the literal meaning of the Word and some sermons based on it, once they get over their astonishment at being in a body and enjoying all the senses they had in the world, and at seeing familiar things around them, they find themselves wanting to know what heaven and hell are like and where they are. So their friends tell them about what eternal life is like and take them around to various places and into the company of different people. They go to different cities, to gardens and parks, often to spectacular ones because things like that appeal to the outer self. Then from time to time they are guided into the thoughts they had during their physical lives about the state of the soul after death and about heaven and hell. This makes them upset that they were so thoroughly ignorant about such matters—and that the church was too.

Almost all of them want to know whether they will be able to get into heaven. Many of them think they will because they led moral and civil lives in the world. They don't reflect on the fact that evil and good people lead lives that are superficially the same. That is, both kinds of people help others; both go to church, listen to sermons, and pray, all the time utterly unaware

that outward behavior and outward worship mean nothing whatever—that all that really matters is the inner self that gives rise
to these outward actions. Scarcely one person in thousands even
knows what the inner self is or that it is where we must look to
find heaven and the church. Even fewer realize that our intentions and thoughts determine our outward actions, as do the love
and faith that are behind those intentions and thoughts and give
rise to them. Even when people are told this, they don't grasp the
fact that thinking and willing are what make the difference; they
believe instead that all that matter are the words they say and the
deeds they do. Many of the people who are coming into the other
life from the Christian world nowadays are like this.

Eventually, good spirits examine them to determine what
they are like. This is done in various ways because in this first
state evil people can say true things and do good things just the
way good people do. As I have already explained, this is because
superficially their lives appeared to be just as moral, since they
were living under governments and laws; and besides, living that
way gained them a reputation for fairness and honesty, and won
people to their side, and brought them prestige and wealth. But
you can tell evil spirits from good ones very easily by the fact that
the evil ones pay close attention when the conversation is about
superficial things, and little attention when it is about deeper
subjects, about the true and good principles of the church and
heaven. They do hear such things, but without any real attention
or pleasure. You can also identify them by the fact that they con-
sistently turn toward certain regions of the spiritual world, and
when they are left to themselves they follow paths that lead to

those regions. You can tell what kind of love is leading them by observing the regions they face and the paths they follow.

Each of the spirits who arrive from the world is linked up with a particular community in heaven or a particular community in hell. However, this applies only to these newcomers' inner selves, and their inner selves are not apparent to them as long as they are focused on their outer selves. This is because their outer selves cover and conceal their inner selves, especially in the case of people involved in evil. However, their inner selves become fully visible when they arrive in the second state of being, because that is where their inner selves are opened and their outer selves become dormant.

This first state after death lasts a few days for some people, months for others, and a year for still others, but rarely more than a year for anyone. These differences depend on how much the inner self and the outer self of each individual disagree or are in harmony. Everyone's inner and outer selves must act in unison and correspond to one another. In the spiritual world, no one is allowed to think and will in one way and yet at the same time to speak and act in another. Everyone must be an image of his or her affection or love, which means we must be the same on the outside as we are on the inside. This is why the first thing that happens is that the outer self of a spirit is uncovered [by spiritual examination] and reorganized—so that it can correspond to the inner self.

OUR SECOND STATE AFTER DEATH

Our second state of being after death is called a state of our inner self because then we are brought fully into the deeper reaches of our minds, or of our will and thoughts, while the more outward interests that engaged us in the first state become dormant.

Anyone who is observant of our life and our words and actions can recognize that we all have an outer self and an inner self, or (to put it another way) superficial thoughts and intentions and also deeper ones. We can know this from the fact that if we are involved in civic life, we think about other people in terms of their reputation, or of what we have picked up about them when they were the subjects of conversation. However, our manner of talking to them can be quite different from our opinion of them. And even if they are evil people, we still behave courteously toward them. This is particularly noticeable in fakers and flatterers whose words and actions are completely different from their thoughts and intentions, and in hypocrites who talk about God, heaven, the salvation of souls, the truths of the church, the welfare of their country, and their neighbor as though they were motivated by faith and love, when at heart they believe in something else and love no one but themselves.

We may gather from this that we have two thought processes, one that is superficial and one that is deeper in us, and that the words we say come from our superficial thinking; but our feelings, which are something else altogether, come from our deeper thoughts. Furthermore, these two thought processes have been separated, because care must be taken to prevent the inner from flowing into the outer and becoming visible in some way.

It is important to know that what we are really like is determined entirely by what our inner self is like, not by what we are like superficially, apart from that inner self. This is because our inner self is our spirit, and since it is from the spirit that the body lives, our life is the life of our spirit. So whatever we are like in our inner self, that is what we are like to eternity. Since our outer self belongs to the body, it is separated after death. Any element of it that does cling to the spirit becomes dormant, serving the deeper self only as an outer level [of the spirit].

We can see from this what really belongs to us and what does not. The fact is that in evil people, the contents of the outer thought that gives rise to their words, and of the outer will that gives rise to their actions, do not really belong to them at all. What belongs to them is the contents of their deeper thought and will.

Once the first state has been completed—the state in which we focus on the outer self, as described in the previous chapter—we are brought to enter fully, as spirits, into the state in which we focus on our inner self. This second state is the one we had in the world with respect to our inner will and the thoughts it produced in us, during the time when we were on our own and our thinking ran free and without control.

We slip into this second state without realizing it, much as we did in the world, when we draw our thoughts, which are the direct source of our speech, back toward our inner self, and let them remain there a while. So when we are in this state as spirits, we are being ourselves and living our real life, since thinking freely, on the basis of what we have affection for, is in fact our true life and our true self.

The thinking of spirits in this state comes from their own will, and so it comes from their own real affection or their own real love; and when that is the case, their thinking joins with their will so closely that they scarcely seem to be thinking of what they do at all, but instead seem to be using only their power of will. It is almost the same when such spirits talk, except that they are concerned that the thoughts that come directly from their will might appear without any covering, since their civic life in the world had planted this fear in their will.

All of us, without exception, are brought into this state after death because it is our own true spiritual state. The earlier state, when we focus on the outer self, was characteristic of our spirit when we were in the company of others. That is not our spirit's own true state, as we can see for several reasons. For example, not only do the thoughts of spirits come directly out of what they love, but so do the things they say, because in the case of spirits, their love is the real source of their speech. It was similar when we engaged in our own private thoughts in the world, because then we did not think in terms of words that we physically uttered, but simply visualized things—and at the same time we thought many more things in a minute than we could say in half an hour.

Another way we can see that this first state that is focused on the outer self is not our own true spiritual state is by considering that when we are in the company of others in the world, we keep what we say in line with the laws of moral and civic life. Then our deeper thinking restrains our outer thinking the way one person restrains another to make sure that the other does not cross the bounds of propriety and decency.

Another indication of this fact is that when we do think privately, we think about what we will say and do in order to please people and to gain friends, good will, and gratitude, and how to do all this by means that are actually foreign to us—that is, how to do this differently than we would if we were just acting on the basis of what we truly want to do.

We can see from all this that the state that spirits are led into next, which is focused on the inner self, is their own true state, which means that it was also the true personal state of those individuals when they were living in the world.

When spirits are in the state that is focused on their inner selves, then it is obvious what kind of people they really were in the world. They actually base their behavior on what they really are. People whose inner self was devoted to good in the world then behave sanely and wisely—more wisely than when they were living in the world, in fact, because they have been freed from any connection with the body and therefore with the earthly things that confuse us and put a kind of cloud between us and reality.

By contrast, people who were focused on evil in the world then behave foolishly and insanely—more insanely than when they were in the world, in fact, because they are free and no longer restrained. As long as they were living in the world, they were superficially sensible, because this was how they imitated rational people. So when the outer layers are stripped off, their inner insanity is unveiled.

An evil person who makes a superficial show of being good can be compared to a brightly polished jar, capped with a lid, in which filth of all kinds is hidden. As the Lord said: "You are like tombs that have been painted white. They look beautiful on the outside, but inside they are full of dead people's bones and filth of every kind" (Matthew 23:27).

To all the people who have led good lives in the world and have acted in accordance with their consciences—that is, people who have acknowledged the Divine Being and loved divine truths, and especially people who have applied them to their lives—it seems that they have awakened from sleep when they are brought into the state that is focused on the inner self. They feel like people who have come from darkness into light. Their thoughts are actually set in motion by heaven's light and therefore by a deeper wisdom, and their actions by what is good and therefore by an inner affection. Heaven is flowing into their thoughts and emotions with an inner blessedness and pleasure that they have never known before. This is because they are in touch with heaven's angels. Then too, they acknowledge the Lord and worship him with their very lives, because they are in their own true lives when they are in the state in which they focus on their inner selves. They are also acknowledging and worshiping him in a state of freedom, since that is what our inner affection gives us. In this way they move away from an outer holiness and into the inner holiness that is the essence of real worship. This is the state of people who have lived a Christian life in accordance with the principles provided by the Word.

Quite the opposite, though, is the state of people who in the world led lives focused on evil, who had no conscience and therefore denied the Divine Being, since all those who live in evil deny the Divine Being inwardly, no matter how convinced they are outwardly that they are not denying but acknowledging him. This is because acknowledging the Divine Being and living in evil are opposites. When people like this in the other life come into the state that focuses on the inner self, they seem foolish to others who hear them talk or see them act, because their evil impulses force them to break out into wicked deeds—into contempt for others, into jeering and blasphemy, hatred, and vengefulness. They cook up plots, some of them with such ingenuity and malice that you would scarcely believe anything like this existed in any human being. They are then free to act in accordance with the thoughts of their will because they are separated from the outer self that restrained them in the world. In short, they lose their ability to reason, because in the world that ability was not located in their inner but in their outer self. Still, to themselves they seem to be wiser than anyone else.

Once people like this are in the second state, they are sent back and forth repeatedly between the state of their outer selves and a recollection of how they behaved when they were in the state of their inner selves. Some of them feel ashamed and admit that they were insane. Some of them are not ashamed at all. Some of them resent the fact that they are not allowed to be in the state of their outer self all the time, but they are shown what they would be like if they were constantly in this state. They would be constantly trying to do the same things covertly, misleading people of simple heart and faith by faking goodness, honesty, and fairness. They would destroy themselves completely, because eventually their outer selves would be ablaze with the same fire as their inner selves; and this would eat up their whole life.

When spirits are in this second state, they actually look exactly the way their inner selves were in the world. The things they had done and said in secret are made public, too, because now they say the same things openly, since no consideration for the outside world is restraining them, and they also keep trying to do what they did before, but now without any of the anxiety they had in the world about their reputations. Furthermore, they are then brought into many of the states that belong to their particular evils, so that angels and good spirits will see them as the people they really are.

This is how hidden things are brought to light and how secrets are exposed. As the Lord said: "Nothing is hidden that will not be revealed, and nothing concealed that will not become known. Whatever you have said in the dark will be heard in the light, and what you have spoken in someone's ear in your rooms will be proclaimed on the rooftops" (Luke 12:2–3). And in another passage: "I say to you that for every idle word people have spoken, they will give an account of it on the day of judgment" (Matthew 12:36).

Every individual goes to the community where her or his spirit was in the world. As I mentioned, each of us is actually united in spirit to some community, either heavenly or hellish— evil people to hellish communities and good people to heavenly ones. Spirits are led toward their communities by stages and finally enter them. When evil spirits are in the state that focuses on the inner self, they gradually turn toward their own communities, and before this state has been brought to a close they are facing them directly.

When the second state has ended, then the evil spirits hurl themselves into a hell where there are people of like mind. To an observer, this plunge looks like that of someone falling backward head first. The reason it looks this way is that the arrangement of the inner self in such people is inverted, since they have loved hellish things and spurned heavenly ones. During this second state, some evil people go in and out of various hells, and while doing so they do not seem to fall headlong the way people do when the process of their spiritual devastation has been completed.

The actual community where their spirits were in the world is shown to them, too, while they are in the state that focuses on the outer self, so that they realize that they were in hell during their physical life. But they were not in the same state as the people who are in hell itself; rather, they were in a state like that of people in the world of spirits.

The separation of evil spirits from good spirits takes place in this second state, since in the first state they were all together. The reason is that as long as spirits are focused on their outer selves it is like the situation in the world—evil people are together with good ones, and good people with evil ones. It is different when people have been brought into their inner self and are left to follow their own true character or will.

This separation of evil people from good ones occurs in various ways. Often the evil are led around to the communities they had been in touch with through their good thoughts and affections during the first state. This brings them to communities they had misled into believing that they were not evil by adopting the outward appearance of goodness. Often they are led around in a large circuit, and good spirits everywhere are shown what they are really like. The good spirits turn away as soon as they see them; and in the same way that the good spirits turn away, the evil spirits who are being led around turn away too, facing the hellish community where they are going.

I will not go into the other ways that the separation of good people from evil people takes place. There are many of them.

OUR THIRD STATE AFTER DEATH

Our third state after death, or the third state of our spirits, is one of instruction. This state is for people who are entering heaven and becoming angels, but not for people who are entering hell, because these latter cannot be taught. As a result, their second state is also their third, and ends in their turning straight toward their own love and therefore toward the hellish community that is engaged in a love like their own. Once this has happened, that love becomes the source of their willing and thinking; and since it is a hellish love, they will to do only what is evil and they think only what is false. They take pleasure in willing and thinking in this way because doing so is a part of what they love. Their finding pleasure in this way results in their rejecting every bit of good and truth they had previously adopted because they thought that it might serve their love as a means to an end.

Good people, though, are brought from the second state into a third, which is a state of preparation for heaven by means of instruction. In fact, no one can be prepared for heaven except by knowing firsthand what is good and true, and that requires being taught. Without being taught, no one can know what spiritual good and truth are, or know the evil and falsity that are their opposites. When we are in the world, it is possible for us to know what civic and moral good and truth are, and what is called fair and honest, because there are civic laws there that teach what is fair, and there are also social situations where we learn to live by moral laws, all of which are based on what is honest and right. Spiritual good and truth, however, are not learned from the world but from heaven. We can in fact know them from the Word and from church doctrine based on the Word, but spiritual good and truth still cannot flow into our lives unless we are in heaven with respect to the deeper levels of our minds. We are in heaven when we acknowledge the Divine Being and at the same time act fairly and honestly, recognizing that we should do so because the Word commands us to. In this way we live fairly and honestly for the sake of the Divine and do not make ourselves and the world our primary goals.

However, no one can behave in this way without first having been taught things like the fact that God exists, that heaven and hell are real, that there is a life after death, that we should love God above all and love our neighbor as we love ourselves, and that we should believe what it says in the Word because the Word is divine. Without recognizing and admitting these principles, we cannot think spiritually. And without thinking about such matters we cannot will to do them, because we cannot think about something if we do not even know of it, and we cannot will to do something that we are not even thinking about. But when we do will such things, heaven flows in—that is, the Lord flows into our lives through heaven, because he flows into our will, and through that into our thought, and through both of these into the way we live, since will and thought are where our entire life comes from. We can see from this that spiritual good and truth are not learned from the world but from heaven, and that no one can be prepared for heaven except by instruction.

Then too, to the extent that the Lord flows into our lives on earth he does teach us here as well, since to that same extent he kindles our will with a love of learning what is true, and enlightens our thought so that we know what is true. To the extent that this happens, our inner self is opened and heaven is sown in it. Even beyond this, to that same extent what is divine and heavenly flows into the honest actions of our moral life, and into the fair actions of our civic life, and makes them spiritual, since the source of our actions is the Divine—because we are doing them *for the sake of* the Divine. The honest and fair actions of our moral and civic life that come from this source are actually the results of our spiritual life; and a result gets everything it is from the thing that causes it, because what the cause is like determines what the results are like.

The teaching is done by angels from a number of communities, mainly those in the northern and southern regions. These angels are focused on intelligence and wisdom based on firsthand knowledge of what is good and true.

The teaching sites are in the north. There are various kinds, differentiated and arranged according to the types and subtypes of heavenly good, so that everyone can be taught there in a manner suited to his or her character and ability to learn. The sites are spread out over a large area in that region.

Good spirits who need to be taught are taken there by the Lord after their second state in the world of spirits has ended. This does not apply to everyone, though, since people who have been taught in the world have already been prepared for heaven by the Lord and are taken up into heaven by a different route. For some, this happens immediately after death. For others, it happens after a short stay with good spirits, during which they are purified by the removal of the coarser elements of their thoughts and affections, elements they picked up from an interest in rank and wealth while they were in the world. Some people go through a process of being spiritually shattered first, which happens in sites called "the lower earth." Some in that place undergo hardships—these would be the people who have convinced themselves of false principles but have still lived good lives. The fact is that false convictions cling tightly to our minds, and until they are dispelled, we cannot see truths, and therefore cannot accept them.

The people who are at these instructional sites reside apart from one another. Their inner selves are individually connected with the communities of heaven they are headed for; and since heaven's communities are arranged in a pattern befitting heaven, so too are the sites where the teaching takes place. As a result, when you look at these sites from heaven, they look like heaven in reduced form. In length they stretch from east to west, and in breadth from south to north.

The general arrangement is as follows.

Toward the front are people who died in childhood and were educated in heaven up to the age of early adolescence. Women instruct them during their childhood, and then they are brought to this location by the Lord and taught here.

Behind these, and farther to the north, there are sites for the instruction of various non-Christian people. In the world they lived good lives in accordance with their own religion, acquired some degree of conscience, and behaved fairly and honestly. They did so not because of the laws of their nation, but because of the laws of their religion, since they believed that these laws were to be reverently obeyed and that nothing they did should violate them. All of these people are readily brought to recognize the Lord when they have been taught to do so, because at heart they believed that God is not invisible but visible in human form.

The non-Christians outnumber all the others in the instructional sites. Those from Africa are especially good people.

Not everyone is taught in the same way or by the same communities of heaven. People who have been raised in heaven from infancy are taught by angels of the inner heavens because they have not absorbed false ideas from distorted religions or polluted their spiritual life with the residue of rank and wealth in the world.

Most people who have died as adults are taught by angels of the outermost heaven because these angels are better suited to them than are the angels of the heavens farther in. The latter—that is, the more inward angels—focus on a deeper wisdom that the deceased cannot yet accept.

Teaching in the heavens differs from teaching on earth because information there is not incorporated into one's memory but into one's way of life, since spirits' memory is in their life. They take in and retain whatever agrees with their way of life and do not take in, much less retain, whatever does not agree with it. This is because spirits actually *are* affections, and so they are in a human form that resembles their affections.

Since this is the way they are, they are constantly inspired with a desire to know what is true so that they can put it to use in their lives. The Lord in fact sees to it that they love doing the useful things that suit their personal gifts. That love is intensified by their hope of becoming angels.

Furthermore, everything done in heaven is focused on each person's being of use for one shared goal, which is the good of the Lord's kingdom (which now is their country). Since all angels there are useful in their own distinctive ways to the extent that the things they do are focused directly and personally on that common usefulness, each and every one of the countless distinctive and individual uses they fulfill is good and heavenly. This means that for each of these spirits their affection for what is true is so closely joined to their affection for usefulness that the two affections act together. A true understanding of usefulness is sown in them in this way, so that the truths they learn are truths about what is useful. This is how angelic spirits are taught and prepared for heaven.

There are various teaching methods (many of them unknown in the world) by which an affection for the truth, suited to each

person's own particular usefulness, is instilled in these individuals. Most of these methods involve representations of useful activities. Such representations can be shown in thousands
of ways in the spiritual world, and they are so enjoyable and
engaging that they soak deep into these spirits, passing all the
way from the deeper levels of their minds to the outer levels of
their bodies. In this way the representations have an effect on
the entire person.

The result is that spirits virtually *become* the useful activities
they personally do. So when they arrive in the communities for
which their instruction has prepared them and begin engaging
in those useful activities, they are fully living the lives that are
theirs alone.

We may gather from this that knowledge in itself, which
is an outward form of truth, does not get anyone into heaven.
Rather, what gets us in is the useful life that is granted through
knowledge.

After spirits have been prepared for heaven at these learning
sites (which does not take long, because they are immersed in
spiritual ideas, which efficiently cover many separate concepts
at once), they are dressed in angelic clothing, which is usually
as white as if it were made of fine linen. Then they are taken to
a path that leads up toward heaven and turned over to guard-
ian angels there. After this they are received by other angels and
acquainted with [various] communities and the great number
of blessings in them. The Lord then takes each person to her or
his own community. This happens by various paths, sometimes

through round-about routes. No angel knows the paths along which they are taken, only the Lord. When they arrive at their own communities, their inner selves are opened, and since they are in harmony with the inner selves of the angels who are members of that community, they are recognized instantly and received with joy.

I would like to add here something remarkable about the paths that lead from these sites to heaven, the paths by which newly arrived angels are admitted. There are eight paths, two from each teaching site. One leads up toward the east and the other toward the west. People who are entering the Lord's heavenly kingdom are admitted by the eastern path, while people who are entering the Lord's spiritual kingdom are admitted by the western path.

The four paths that lead to the Lord's heavenly kingdom are adorned with olive trees and various fruit trees, while the ones that lead to the Lord's spiritual kingdom are adorned with grapevines and laurel. These are correspondences: vines and laurel correspond to an affection for truth and how it is used, while olive and fruit trees correspond to an affection for what is good and how that is used.

IT IS NOT AS HARD AS PEOPLE THINK IT IS
TO LIVE A LIFE THAT LEADS TO HEAVEN

Some people believe it is hard to live a life that leads to heaven, the kind of life that is called "spiritual," because they have heard that they need to renounce the world, give up the desires associated with the body and the flesh, and "live spiritually." Specifically, they think, this means they will have to reject worldly things, especially money and prestige, and go around in constant, pious meditation about God, salvation, and eternal life, devoting their lives to prayer, and reading the Word and religious literature. This is what they call renouncing the world and living for the spirit and not for the flesh.

However, the actual case is quite different, as I have learned from an abundance of experience and conversation with angels. In fact, people who renounce the world and live for the spirit in this fashion only get themselves a depressing life, a life that cannot experience the joy in heaven, since our life remains with us after death. No, if we are going to gain a life in heaven, we absolutely must live in the world and take part in its duties and its business. This is how we gain a spiritual life—by means of our moral and civic life. There is no other way a spiritual life can be formed within us, no other way our spirits can be prepared for heaven. This is because living an inner life and not an outer life at the same time is like living in a house that has no foundation: it gradually settles, develops gaping cracks, and sways until it collapses.

If we look at human life and examine it with the insights granted us by our power of reasoning, it turns out to be three-fold. It is made up of spiritual life, moral life, and civic life. These lives can be seen to be different: some people live a civic life but not a moral or spiritual one, some live a moral life but not a spiritual one, and some live a civic and a moral life and a spiritual life as well. These last are the people who are leading the life of heaven, while the others are leading the world's life, which is disconnected from the life of heaven.

The primary thing that emerges from this discussion is that a spiritual life is not without connection to physical life—life in the world—but is joined to it in the way a soul is joined to its body. If a spiritual life were without that connection, it would be like the house without a foundation that was just described.

In fact, our moral and civic living is the driving force behind our spiritual life, because *willing to do good* is the essence of spiritual life, and *doing good actions* is the essence of moral and civic life. If willing is disconnected from action, spiritual life becomes mere thinking, mere talking, and the power of the will falls away—because it has nothing to rest on. Our will is our actual spiritual being.

What follows will make it possible for anyone to see that it is not as hard as people think it is to live a life that leads to heaven.

Is there anyone who can't live in a moral and civil fashion? After all, we start off doing so in infancy, and living in the world teaches us how. We live in this way whether we are evil or good, since no one wants to be called dishonest or unfair. Almost all people behave honestly and fairly outwardly, even to the point of seeming genuinely honest and fair—that is, seeming to base their actions on real honesty and fairness. Spiritual people are called upon to live in the same way and can do so just as easily as worldly people. But the difference is that spiritual people believe in the Divine Being and act honestly and fairly not just because by doing so they are following civic and moral laws, but also because they are following divine laws. In fact, since they are thinking about divine laws when they act, they are in touch with heaven's angels; and to the extent that they are in touch with those angels, they are united to them, and their inner self— which is essentially a spiritual person—is made active. When this is how we are, the Lord adopts and leads us without our realizing it, and the things we do that are honest and fair—the actions of our moral and civic life—come from a spiritual source. When an honest and fair action comes from a spiritual source, it comes from genuine honesty and fairness. It comes from the heart.

On the outside, such honesty and fairness look just like the honesty and fairness of worldly people or even evil and hellish people, but the inner form of those qualities is totally different. Evil people do what is fair and honest purely for their own sake and for worldly reasons. If they were not afraid of the law and its penalties, and of losing their reputation, their wealth, and their life, they would act with utter dishonesty and unfairness. Since they have no fear of God or of any divine law, they have no inner restraint that keeps them in check; so they cheat and rob and plunder others as much as they can, for the sheer pleasure of it. It is especially clear that their inner selves are this way if we compare them to people who are like them in the other life. There the outer selves of all are stripped away and the inner selves are activated—the selves with which such people will go on living to eternity. Since evil people are then acting without external restraints, which are (as was just pointed out) fear of the law and fear of losing reputation, prestige, profit, and life, their actions are deranged, and they scoff at honesty and fairness.

By contrast, people who have lived honestly and fairly because they are obeying divine laws will act wisely when their outer selves are stripped away and they are left only with their inner selves. They are then united to heaven's angels, who share their wisdom with them.

One thing that should now be clear from all this is that spiritual people may seem to behave in much the same way as worldly people in their civic and moral life, but they are united to the Divine in their inner selves, in their will and thought.

The laws of spiritual life, the laws of civic life, and the laws of moral life are handed down to us in the Ten Commandments.

The first three commandments contain the laws of spiritual life, the next four the laws of civic life, and the last three the laws of moral life. Outwardly, the people who are merely worldly live by these commandments just the way spiritual people do. They worship the Divine in the same way: they go to church, listen to sermons, and compose themselves for their devotions. They do not kill or commit adultery or steal or bear false witness, do not cheat their companions of their goods. However, they behave this way solely in their own interest, in order to look good in the world. Inwardly, these same people are exactly the opposite of what they seem to be outwardly. Because at heart they deny the Divine, they play the hypocrite in their worship. In their private thinking they scoff at the holy rites of the church, believing that they serve only to restrain the unsophisticated masses. This is why they are totally cut off from heaven.

So since they are not spiritual, they are not moral or civic people either: even though they do not kill, they hate everyone who gets in their way, and their hatred makes them burn to take revenge. If they were not bound by civic laws and the outward restraints caused by their fears, they would kill.

But by craving to kill, they are constantly killing.

Even though they do not commit adultery, they are constantly adulterous all the same, because they believe there is nothing wrong with it. They actually do commit it as much as they can and as often as they have the opportunity.

Even though they do not actually steal, they are constantly meaning to steal all the same, since they covet other people's assets and think of cheating and malicious fraud as legally justifiable.

The same applies to the other commandments of moral life—not bearing false witness or coveting the goods of others. All who deny the Divine are like this, all who do not have some conscience based on religion. It is obvious that this is the way their inner selves are if we compare them to people who are like them in the other life, after those spirits have had their outer selves stripped away and are brought fully into their inner selves. Since they are cut off from heaven at that point, they act in league with hell and keep company with the people there.

It is different for people who in their hearts acknowledged the Divine Being and paid attention to divine laws in what they did in the world, keeping not only the first three of the Ten Commandments but the others as well. When they are brought fully into their inner self, after their outer self is stripped away, they are wiser than they were in the world. Coming into their inner selves is like coming from darkness into light, from ignorance into wisdom, from a sad life into a blissful one, because they are in the Divine and therefore in heaven.

I have described all this so that it can be seen what each of these two types of people is like, though both may lead the same kind of outward life.

Anyone can see that thoughts tend to follow where intentions lead, or to go where we aim them. Thought is actually our inner sight, and it behaves like our outer sight. It shifts toward and rests on whatever it is turned toward and aimed at. If our inner sight or thought is turned toward the world and rests on that, the result is that our thought becomes worldly. If it is turned toward our selves and our prestige, it becomes materialistic. However, if it is turned toward heaven, it becomes heavenly. So if it is turned toward heaven, it is raised up; if it is turned toward our selves, it is pulled away from heaven and immersed in the physical; if it is turned toward the world, it is also turned away from heaven and dispersed among whatever objects meet our eyes.

It is our love that creates our intentions and focuses our inner sight, or our thought, on its objects. This is why love for ourselves directs our thought toward ourselves and whatever we call our own, while love of the world directs it toward worldly matters, and love of heaven directs it toward heavenly matters. From this fact we can tell what state our inner minds are in— all we need to do is to identify what we love. That is, if we love heaven, the inner reaches of our minds are raised up toward heaven and open upward. If we love the world and ourselves, the inner reaches of our minds are closed in the upward direction and instead open toward outer things. So it's clear that if the higher reaches of our minds are closed to what is above them, we can no longer see whatever has to do with heaven and the church. As far as we are concerned, those things lie in darkness; and whatever is in darkness we either deny or at least do not understand. This is why people who love themselves and the world above all, since the higher levels of their minds are closed, in their hearts deny divine truths; and even if they do speak about them from rote memory, they still do not understand what they are saying. They have the same attitude toward divine truths as they do toward worldly and material things. Because this is the way they are, they cannot think about anything except what comes in through their physical senses, which for them are the sole source of pleasure. Their sensory experience also includes much that is foul, obscene, irreligious, and criminal. They cannot be distracted from these obsessions because there is no inflow from heaven into their minds, since as just mentioned their minds are closed to what is above them.

Our intention is our will. This is what focuses our inner sight or thought, since what we want, we form an intention to get; and what we intend to get, we think about. So if we form an intention to go to heaven, we focus our thinking on that, and with our thinking we focus our whole mind, which as a result is in heaven. This means that our mind looks at the concerns of the world as below itself, like someone looking down from the roof of a house. This is why people in whom the deeper levels of the mind are open can see the evil and false elements in themselves, since these are below their spiritual mind. Conversely, if people's inner selves are not open, they cannot see those evil and false elements because they are right down among them and not above them. This shows us where human wisdom comes from, and human insanity too, and what we will be like after death when we are left to will and think and then to act and speak in keeping with our inner self.

Again, this discussion has been included to indicate what a person is like inside, and that it does not matter how similar to someone else she or he may seem outwardly.

We can now see that it is not as hard to lead the life of heaven as people think. It is simply a matter of recognizing that when we encounter something that we know is dishonest or unfair, no matter how tempting it is we are not to do it, because it is against the divine commandments. If we get used to thinking like this, and from this familiarity form a habit, then we are gradually united to heaven. The more we are united to heaven, the more the higher levels of our minds are opened, and the more they are opened, the more we perceive what is dishonest or unfair in ourselves; and the more we can identify these qualities, the more we can remove them. The fact is that no evil can be done away with until we can see it.

It is our freedom that allows us to first enter into this state of being in heaven, since everyone is free to think in this way. However, once the process has started, the Lord works his wonders within us and causes us not only to see evils but also to not want them, and eventually to turn away from them. This is the meaning of the Lord's words, "My yoke is easy and my burden light" (Matthew 11:30).

It is important to realize, though, that the difficulty of thinking like this and also of resisting evils increases the more we deliberately do evil things—in fact, the more we become used to doing them and ultimately no longer see them. Then we come to love them and to excuse them to gratify our love, and to rationalize them with all kinds of self-deceptions and say we are allowed to do them, that they are good. This happens to people who in early adulthood plunge into all kinds of evil without restraint and at the same time reject everything divine with all their hearts.

I was once shown the way to heaven and the way to hell. There was a broad path leading off to the left or north. A great many spirits could be seen traveling along it. In the distance, however, I could see a fairly large boulder where the broad path ended. Two paths led away from the boulder; one went to the left, and the other, which was on the other side of the stone, went to the right. The path to the left was narrow and confined, leading around through the west to the south, and therefore into the light of heaven. The path to the right was broad and open, leading on a slant downwards toward hell.

At first—up to the large boulder at the fork—everyone could be seen to be following the same path; but at that point they parted company. The good turned to the left and started along the confined path that led to heaven. The evil did not even see the boulder at the fork but fell over it and hurt themselves. When they got up, they hurried along the broad path to the right that led toward hell.

Later the meaning of all this was explained to me. The first path, the broad one where many good people and many evil people were traveling together—all chatting with one another like friends, because they could not see the differences between them—that path represented people who live similarly honest and fair outward lives, and who cannot be told apart from the way they look. The stone at the fork or corner where the evil people stumbled, from which they hurried along the path to hell, represented divine truth, which is denied by people who are focusing on hell. In the highest sense, this stone meant the Lord's divine human nature. However, people who acknowledged divine truth, and the divine nature of the Lord as well, were taken along the path that led to heaven.

This showed me again that both evil and good people live the same life outwardly, or travel the same path, one as readily as the other. Yet the ones who in their hearts acknowledge the Divine, especially those within the church who acknowledge the Lord's divine nature, are led to heaven. Those who do not acknowledge it are led to hell.

Paths in the other life represent the thoughts that flow from our will, or intention. The paths that are visible there answer exactly to the thoughts that arise from our intentions. And we walk wherever the thoughts lead us that arise from our intentions. This is why you can tell from the paths spirits take what they and their thoughts are like.

Seeing the broad and narrow paths taught me the meaning of the Lord's words, "Enter through the narrow gate, for wide is the gate and open the way that leads to destruction, and there are many who walk along it; confined is the path and narrow the gate that leads to life, and there are few who find it" (Matthew 7:13–14). The way that leads to life is narrow not because it is difficult. Instead it is narrow because so few people find it, as has been mentioned.

The boulder I saw at the corner where the broad, common path ended and from which the two ways seemed to lead in opposite directions showed me the meaning of the Lord's words, "Have you not read what is written, 'The stone that the builders rejected has become the main cornerstone'? Whoever falls over this stone will be shattered" (Luke 20:17–18). The stone means divine truth, and the rock of Israel [2 Samuel 23:3] means the Lord in regard to his divine human nature. The builders are the people of the church. The main cornerstone is where the fork is, and to fall and be shattered is to deny and perish.

I have been allowed to talk with some people in the other life who had distanced themselves from the affairs of the world in order to lead pious and holy lives, and also with some who had mortified themselves in various ways because they thought this was renouncing the world and taming the desires of the flesh. However, all that most of them got from this was a depressing existence. They had distanced themselves from a life of active kindness, which we can have only by taking part in the world. As a result, they could not associate with angels, because the life of angels—which is cheerful and blessed—consists of doing good, of actions done out of loving kindness for others.

To make matters worse, people who have led a life apart from the world are on fire with a sense of self-righteousness and constantly crave heaven. They think of heavenly joy as their reward, but they have no knowledge whatever of what heavenly joy actually is. In fact, the joy of angels has no sense of self-righteousness in it. It consists of work and of public duties and of bliss at the good that is accomplished through these things. When people who have led a life apart are brought together with angels and are allowed to share in their joy, they are as bewildered as though they were seeing something totally alien to their faith. Since they cannot respond to that joy, they go away and associate with people who led the same kind of life in the world as they did.

I have discussed all this to show that the life that leads to heaven is not one of withdrawal *from* the world but of living *in* the world, and that living piously but without loving kindness (and we can act with loving kindness only by taking part in the world) does not lead to heaven at all.

No, the life that leads to heaven is a life of loving kindness. It is a life of behaving honestly and fairly in every duty, every business transaction, every task, acting from our deeper self and therefore from a heavenly source. This source is operating in the way we live our lives whenever we act honestly and fairly specifically because doing so is in accordance with divine laws.

The life that leads to heaven is not hard. A life of piety apart from a life of loving kindness is hard. And just as surely as people believe it leads to heaven, it doesn't. It leads away from there.

CHILDREN IN HEAVEN

Some people believe that only children born in the church get into heaven, not children born outside the church. They say this is because children born in the church are baptized and are introduced into the faith of the church by their baptism. What they don't realize is that being baptized doesn't give people faith or get them into heaven. Baptism serves only as a sign and reminder that we need to be regenerated, and that people born in the church can be regenerated because the Word is there, the Word that contains the divine truths that make regeneration possible. The church is where the Lord, who is the source of regeneration, is known.

So these people should realize that every child who dies, no matter where he or she was born, within the church or outside it, of devout or irreverent parents, is accepted by the Lord after death, brought up in heaven, taught according to the divine design, and filled with affection for what is good and through that with direct knowledge of the truth; and then, being continually perfected in intelligence and wisdom, all such individuals are led into heaven and become angels.

Anyone who thinks rationally can realize that no one is born to go to hell—everyone is born to go to heaven. We ourselves are to blame if we arrive in hell, but children are not yet liable for any blame.

Children who die are still children in the other life. They have the same kind of childlike mind, the same unknowing innocence, the same tenderness toward all. But they are only just beginning to be able to become angels; they are not angels but only angels-to-be.

Actually, everyone who leaves this world is [at first] in the same state of life—a baby is in the state of a baby, a child in the state of a child, an adolescent or adult or senior in the state of an adolescent, an adult, or a senior. This state does, of course, eventually change. A child's state is better than the others, though, because a child is innocent, and because children have not yet let evils take root in them by actually living them. Because of the nature of innocence, every heavenly thing can be sown in it; it is able to contain the truths that make our faith and the good that comes from love.

The condition of children in the other life is vastly better than that of children in our world because they are not clothed with an earthly body. Instead, they have an angelic one. An earthly body is inherently heavy. It does not receive its primary sensations and primary impulses from the inner or spiritual world but from the outer or material one; so children in this world have to learn through practice to walk, to do things, and to talk—even their senses, such as sight and hearing, are developed by use. It is different for children in the other life. Because they are spirits, their actions arise directly from their inner selves. They walk without practice and even talk, though at first they speak only on the basis of miscellaneous emotions that are not yet differentiated into mental concepts. However, since their outer selves are essentially the same as their inner selves, they very soon begin using mental concepts [in their speech] as well. The fact is that angels' speech is in perfect agreement with the thoughts that arise from their emotions, not only because their speech flows from those emotions, but because their emotions take on their own varied coloration from their mental concepts.

As soon as children are reawakened (which happens immediately after their death), they are taken to heaven and entrusted to female angels who loved children tenderly during their physical lives and loved God as well. Since in this world they loved all children as tenderly as if they had been mothers to them, they accept these new ones as their own, and the children instinctively love them as their mothers. Each such angel has as many children as her spiritual maternal nature wants.

I need to explain briefly how children are brought up in heaven. They learn to speak from their teachers. Their first speech is only a sound produced by emotion. It gradually becomes more articulate as the concepts they are thinking enter into it, since concepts of this kind that arise from emotions make up the whole angelic language.

The kinds of things children see with their eyes that particularly delight them are the first objects associated with these emotions, which are totally innocent in origin. Since everything they see is from a spiritual source, aspects of heaven flow into them that open their deeper selves. In this way they grow closer to perfection every day. Once this first stage has been completed, they are taken to another heaven where they are taught by instructors, and so on.

They are taught in particular by images suited to their characters, images that are unbelievably beautiful and full of a wisdom that comes from within. In this way there is gradually instilled into them an intelligence whose very soul comes from what is good.

I may cite at this point two examples I have been allowed to see that will serve to suggest the nature of the rest of these images.

1. The Lord was shown rising from the tomb, and along with this concept was shown the uniting of his human nature with his divine nature. This was done in a manner so wise that it surpassed all human wisdom, but also in a manner both childlike and innocent. For example, though the idea of the tomb was indicated, the idea of the Lord was not shown at the same time, except only so subtly that one could hardly tell that it was the Lord, as though he were far off. They used this device to remove the idea of death that is associated with tombs. Then they very judiciously allowed something misty, something that looked like a thin vapor, to flow into the tomb. By this they were

symbolizing, again with appropriate subtlety, the spiritual life represented by baptism.

2. Then I saw these angels represent the Lord coming down to those who were bound and rising with them into heaven [Psalms 68:18; Ephesians 4:8–10; 1 Peter 3:19–20]. This they showed with incomparable judiciousness and reverence. As a concession to the way children understand things, they supported the Lord in his ascent by small cords they had let down, so slender and sheer as to be almost invisible. Throughout it all, they had a holy fear of letting any part of the representation touch on anything that was not spiritual and heavenly.

There were other representations that engaged the children as well—for example, plays suited to children's minds—through which the children were led into awareness of truth and into an affection for what is good.

I was also shown what their tender understanding is like. When I was saying the Lord's Prayer and they were flowing into my concepts on the basis of their own understanding of it, I noticed that their inflow was so tender and gentle that it was almost nothing but pure feeling. At the same time, I noted that their understanding had been opened to the Lord, for it was as though what was coming from them was flowing through them. In fact, the Lord does flow into children's ideas, primarily from the deepest self. Nothing has closed this off in children, as is the case in adults—no false principles close them off from true understanding, no evil way of life closes them off from accepting what is good and thus from being wise.

Children in Heaven

We can see from all this that immediately after their death children do not enter the state that angels are in, but are gradually brought into that state through growing awareness of what is good and true. This is according to the design of heaven. The smallest details of their characters are known to the Lord, so they are led, in a way that matches each and every impulse of their own inclinations, toward the acceptance of truths that arise from good and the good that is done because of truth.

I have also been shown how everything instilled in them is taught by methods that greatly interest and please the children and suit their personalities. I have been allowed to see, as an example of one of these methods, children exquisitely dressed, wearing garlands of flowers around their necks and slender arms, the blossoms bright with striking and heavenly colors. Once I was also allowed to see some children with their teachers in a garden like paradise, in the company of some young women. It was a garden not of trees, but of something like laurels, shaped into vaulted arches; these formed heavily decorated doorways over paths leading to inner recesses. The children themselves were dressed with comparable beauty. When they went in through the doorways, the flowers over the entrance radiated the most joyous light imaginable. From this one can see what sorts of things give them pleasure. From this, too, one can see how they are guided into the blessings of innocence and loving kindness by things that interest them and please them, which the Lord constantly fills with those blessings.

By a means of communication that is common in the other life, I have been shown what children's concepts are like when they are looking at various objects. It is as though everything were alive; so in the smallest concepts of their thought there is an inherent life. I gathered that children on earth have concepts that are much the same when they are involved in their play, since they are not yet able to reflect, as do grownups, about what is inanimate.

I mentioned earlier that children have either a heavenly or a spiritual nature. You can tell those who are heavenly from those who are spiritual very readily. Heavenly children think and talk and act more gently, so that [the representation] that appears is hardly more than something flowing from a love of what is good, a love for the Lord and for other children.

Spiritual children do not think and talk and act so gently. Instead, [their representation] is something like fluttering wings that are revealed in little things about them. Then too, their difference from heavenly children can be seen in their moodiness, as well as in other matters.

Many people conjecture that children continue as children in heaven and are still like children when they are among the angels. People in ignorance of what an angel is may have had this opinion erroneously confirmed by the images here and there in churches, where angels are represented as children. However, the truth of the matter is actually very different. Intelligence and wisdom make an angel, qualities that children do not have as long as they remain children. Children are with the angels, but they themselves are not angels yet. Once they are intelligent and wise they are angels for the first time. In fact—and this is something that surprised me—then they no longer look like children but like adults, because they no longer have a childlike nature but a more grown-up angelic nature. This goes along with intelligence and wisdom.

The reason children look more grown-up—that is, like adolescents and young adults—as they grow closer to perfection in intelligence and wisdom is that intelligence and wisdom are the essential spiritual food. So the things that nourish their minds also nourish their bodies. This is a result of correspondence, since the form of the body is nothing but an outward form of their inner selves.

It is important to realize that children in heaven do not grow up beyond the prime of youth, but remain at that age forever. To assure me of this, I have been allowed to talk with some who had been raised as children in heaven and had grown up there. To others I spoke while they were still children, and then with the same group later when they had become youths; and I heard from them about the course of their life from one age level to another.

Innocence contains everything heavenly. That is the reason that children's innocence is a basis for all the affections for what is good and true. Innocence is wanting to be led by the Lord and not by oneself, so the more innocent we are, the less preoccupied we are with our self-image. And the more free we are of our preoccupation with our self-image, the more we gain an identity given by the Lord. The Lord's identity is what is called the Lord's righteousness and merit.

Children's innocence, though, is not real innocence, because it still lacks wisdom. Real innocence is wisdom because to the extent that we are wise we want to be led by the Lord; or what amounts to the same thing, to the extent that we love being led by the Lord, we are wise.

So children are brought from the outward innocence that characterizes them at first, which is called the innocence of infancy, to the inner innocence that is the innocence of wisdom. This second innocence is the goal of their whole process of instruction. So when they arrive at the innocence of wisdom, the innocence of infancy that had served them as a basis during this process is joined to them.

The nature of children's innocence was represented to me as something woody and almost lifeless. Then it was brought to life as the children were brought closer to perfection by recognizing truths and beginning to love what is good. After this display, the nature of true innocence was represented to me as a supremely beautiful baby, naked and very much alive; and in fact in the eyes of other angels, the truly innocent people, in the deepest heaven, appear exactly like little children. Some of them are even naked, since innocence is portrayed as a nakedness without embarrassment, as we read concerning the first human and his wife in the garden (Genesis 2:25). So too, when they lost their innocence they were ashamed of their nakedness and hid themselves (Genesis 3:7, 10, 11).

In short, the wiser angels are, the more innocent they are; and the more innocent they are, the more they look to themselves like children. This is why infancy in the Word means innocence.

I have talked with angels about children, and I asked whether they were pure and without evil, reasoning that they did not have any evil that has been carried into action, the way adults do. I was told, though, that they have just as much evil within themselves—that in fact they too are nothing but evil. However, they, like all the angels, are held back from their evil by the Lord and kept focused on what is good, until it seems to them as though they are focused on what is good of their own accord. So to prevent children from having a false notion about themselves after they have grown up in heaven—a belief that the good that surrounds them is from them and not from the Lord—they are placed back in their hereditary evils from time to time and left in them until they know and recognize and believe the way things really are.

There was one individual who had died in infancy and grown up in heaven who had this kind of opinion. He was the son of a particular king; so he was placed back in his own innate life of evil. I could tell then from the aura of his life that he was driven to lord it over others and regarded adultery as of no concern whatever—evils that were part of his heredity from his parents. Once he recognized that he was like this, though, he was welcomed back among the angels he had been with before.

In the other life, none of us ever suffers any punishment for inherited evil, because it is not ours. We are not at fault for our hereditary nature. We suffer punishment for any personal evil we have carried into action—that is, for whatever hereditary evil we have made our own by acting it out in our lives.

The reason grown-up children are placed back in the state of their hereditary evil is not to punish them. It is to make sure they know that on their own they are nothing but evil and that they are carried from the hell in which they are into heaven by the Lord's mercy, that they are in heaven not because they deserve it, but because of the Lord. This prevents them from boasting that they are better than others because of the good that they have. That would be against the goodness of loving one another just as it is against what faith teaches to be true.

Several times a number of children have been with me in choirs, before they had learned to talk at all. They made a faint, disorganized sound, as though they were not yet able to perform in unison the way they would when they were older. But what really surprised me was that the spirits who were with me could not keep from trying to get them to talk—this kind of impulse is innate in spirits. Every time, though, I noticed that the children resisted, not wanting to be compelled to speak in this way. I often picked up a reluctance from them, a distaste that had a kind of resentment in it. When they were granted some power of speech, all they said was "That isn't so." I was told that this is a kind of testing of the children not only to accustom and introduce them to resisting whatever is false and evil but to keep them from thinking or speaking or acting at the bidding of someone else, so that they will not let themselves be led by anyone but the Lord.

We may gather from this what the upbringing of children is like in heaven—through an understanding of truth and a wisdom about what is good, they are led into an angelic life, which consists of love for the Lord and a mutual love that contains innocence.

An example may serve to illustrate how different the upbringing of children on earth is in many instances. I was on the street of a large city and saw some boys fighting with each other. A crowd gathered and watched this with considerable pleasure, and I was told that the parents themselves urged their children into fights like these. The good spirits and angels who were seeing all this through my eyes were so repelled that I could feel them shudder, especially at the fact that the parents were encouraging this kind of behavior. They said that by doing this they would at the very earliest age stifle all the mutual love and all the innocence that little ones receive from the Lord, and that they would lead them into hatred and vindictiveness. So by their own deliberate practices they would shut their children out of heaven, where there is nothing but mutual love. Let any parents who wish well for their children beware of things like this.

I need also to describe the difference between people who die as children and people who die as adults. People who die as adults have a level [in their spirit] acquired from the earthly, material world, and they take it with them. This level is their memory and its material and bodily emotion. After death, content is no longer added to it, and it then becomes inactive; but it still serves their thought after death as an outer level because their thinking flows into it. Thus this level—and the way a person's powers of reasoning correspond to what the level contains—determines what a person is like after death.

People who have died in childhood and have been raised in heaven, though, do not have this kind of level. They have a level that has shifted from the worldly to the spiritual, because they bring with them nothing from the material world or their earthly bodies. This means that they cannot be caught up in the coarse emotions of the world or in the thoughts that come from those emotions. They actually draw on heaven for everything they are.

Not only that, but little children are unaware that they were born on earth, so they think they were born in heaven. This means they do not know what any birth is other than the spiritual birth that is accomplished through familiarity with what is good and true and through the intelligence and wisdom that make people truly human. Since these come from the Lord, they believe that they belong to the Lord himself, and love to have it so.

However, if people who have grown up on earth distance themselves from the love of material and earthly things, from love for themselves and for the world, and take up the love of spiritual things instead, they can approach perfection just as much as do children who have grown up in heaven.

ABOUT EMANUEL SWEDENBORG

Emanuel Swedenborg (1688–1772) was born Emanuel Swedberg (or Svedberg) in Stockholm, Sweden, on January 29, 1688 (Julian calendar). He was the third of the nine children of Jesper Swedberg (1653–1735) and Sara Behm (1666–1696). At the age of eight he lost his mother. After the death of his only older brother ten days later, he became the oldest living son. In 1697 his father married Sara Bergia (1666–1720), who developed great affection for Emanuel and left him a significant inheritance. His father, a Lutheran clergyman, later became a celebrated and controversial bishop, whose diocese included the Swedish churches in Pennsylvania and in London, England.

After studying at the University of Uppsala (1699–1709), Emanuel journeyed to England, Holland, France, and Germany (1710–1715) to study and work with leading scientists in western Europe. Upon his return he apprenticed as an engineer under the brilliant Swedish inventor Christopher Polhem (1661–1751). He gained favor with Sweden's King Charles XII (1682–1718), who gave him a salaried position as an overseer of Sweden's mining industry (1716–1747). Although he was engaged, he never married.

After the death of Charles XII, Emanuel was ennobled by Queen Ulrika Eleonora (1688–1741), and his last name was changed to Swedenborg (or Svedenborg). This change in status gave him a seat in the Swedish House of Nobles, where he remained an active participant in the Swedish government throughout his life.

A member of the Royal Swedish Academy of Sciences, he devoted himself to scientific studies and philosophical reflections that culminated in a number of publications, most notably a comprehensive three-volume work on mineralogy (1734) that brought him recognition across Europe as a scientist and philosopher. After 1734 he redirected his research and publishing to a study of anatomy in search of the interface between the soul and body, making several significant discoveries in physiology.

From 1743 to 1745 he entered a transitional phase that resulted in a shift of his main focus from science and philosophy to theology. Throughout the rest of his life he maintained that this shift was brought about by Jesus Christ, who appeared to him, called him to a new mission, and opened his perception to a permanent dual consciousness of this life and the life after death.

He devoted the last decades of his life to studying Scripture and publishing eighteen theological titles that draw on the Bible, reasoning, and his own spiritual experiences. These works present a Christian theology with unique perspectives on the nature of God, the spiritual world, the Bible, the human mind, and the path to salvation.

Swedenborg died in London on March 29, 1772, at the age of eighty-four.

READ MORE FROM EMANUEL SWEDENBORG

Heaven and Hell (from which *Our Life after Death* was excerpted) is Swedenborg's most popular book and his fullest report of the afterlife, especially appropriate for readers interested in near-death experiences or who seek consolation for the loss of a loved one. This volume, part of our New Century Edition series, is offered in several formats: Deluxe annotated hardcover or paperback (pictured); "Portable" paperback, which includes only the text of the translation; or free download at www.swedenborg.com.

A *Swedenborg Sampler* presents key selections from five New Century Edition volumes, focusing on the afterlife, the nature of God and the spiritual dynamics behind human suffering, new perspectives on Christianity, and inner meanings of the Bible. Available at fine book retailers or through our website.

The Swedenborg Foundation has worked since 1849 to make Emanuel Swedenborg's spiritual vision more widely known. Visit us at **www.swedenborg.com** to read his writings online, peruse our bookstore, and connect through social media with others who are interested in his insights.